THE NATURE OF AESTHETICS

DEFINING LITERATURE, ART & BEAUTY

CHRISTOPHER ANGLE

Second Edition

Copyright ©1995 by Christopher Angle

All rights reserved.

No part of this book may be reproduced or transmitted in any form or by any means, electronic or mechanical, including photocopy, recording, or any information storage or retrieval system, without the express written permission of the publisher, except where permitted by law.

Library of Congress Catalog 95–69184

ISBN 979-8-9877707-0-2

Published by

RITE Report Inc.
100 Research Dr., Suite 16
Stamford, CT 06906
Tel. 203/253-2008
Email: chrisangle1@gmail.com

Contents

The material herein and hereinafter will bear the influence of two teachers of the University of Michigan — Detmar Finke and Frank B. Livingstone.

THE NATURE OF LITERATURE

Detmar is a botany professor at a major university, and being an intellectually well-rounded person, he has a keen interest in the arts, with a special inclination toward philosophy. When it comes to subjects of philosophical concern, we often find Detmar communicating with professors and students alike of the various departments. Also, Detmar seeks and encourages contact with students who by their own initiative suggest new ideas and thoughts to their professors and show a promising interest in philosophy. One of these students, Haskell, appears to be headed for a degree in philosophy and has met Detmar on several occasions. Once again Haskell comes to visit Detmar and appears to have something on his mind.

Haskell enters Detmar's office and greets him. "Detmar! Good afternoon". (Detmar prefers to have the students call him by his Christian name in order to abolish any barriers that would hinder the building of a good rapport.)

DTMR: Haskell, Hi! It's a good afternoon when I get a visit from a friend and one with a good head, too. Please come in and sit down.

HSKL: I'm not disturbing you, am I? I know you're busy with your research.

DTMR: By no means. To what do I owe the pleasure of this visit?

HSKL: Well, this semester I'm not only involved in the study of philosophy courses, but I'm also applying myself to creative writing and English literature courses. I am certainly learning much under the tutelage of my professors; however, lately while listening to some of the explanations of one professor concerning certain famous poems, I have come to wonder in what light the professor examines and interprets these poems. At times he has expounded extensively on the simplest of verses when I cannot help wondering what was the intent of the poem in its entirety.

These instances of listening and reflecting upon my professor's interpretations of poems not only lead me to reflect about any one poem's meaning, but also make me wonder how it is that one should look upon and examine any one poem, or indeed, any one piece of literature. The prolixity of, not only my present English literature professor but of other English literature professors has led me first into confusion and then into wonder that these men of higher learning have not any concrete ideas by which to view literature. They examine works of prose and verse in a superficial manner which leads to generalizations and intellectualizations that I cannot understand and which leave me in doubt as to whether I am learning. These doubts come to me in spite of the fact that these men are all well respected by other men in their field, and by their peers, and by men of much higher intellect than I. Is it a deficiency in me that I am not able to grasp the contents of their lectures?

DTMR: Did you question your professors about the matters which you have presented me?

HSKL: Yes. I have visited my English literature professor, and he proceeded with a harangue that was not understandable to the likes of me. I believe it did not even bear on the subject of how to approach literature. However, my creative writing professor did give me an answer that I believe had some thought behind it, yet it was an answer that could not satisfy me completely.

DTMR: And what was that answer? Please tell me.

HSKL: Basically, he explained that he, as well as many modern critics, views any piece of prose or verse with the following in mind: unity and clarity of expression.

DTMR: And why was this an insufficient answer?

HSKL: It does not denote any difference between the art of literature and a simple newspaper article; they both can have unity and clarity of expression. In fact, those are components of any good writing, whether it be a poem, essay, magazine article, newspaper editorial, or a great novel.

DTMR: I agree with you that what he said is correct, but perhaps it was not quite exclusive enough.

HSKL: How's that?

DTMR: Let us begin an inquiry. It appears to me that we should proceed directly to discerning what literature is and establishing a definition. Once a definition is postulated, we should soon be able to know how to approach any piece of prose or verse which we may want to peruse in an academic manner. But first, in order to establish a definition, we should examine what an author does when he writes; that is, we should determine exactly what is the basic process that occurs in his mind when he puts the pen to the paper.

HSKL: Yes, we should examine that process first.

DTMR: When an author writes, I propose he just writes of his experiences. If he were not to have any experiences, he would not be able to write of the world. Thus, we can see that an author is expressing his own particular view of the world. From this, I submit that literature is the written expression of how the author views his involvement in the world.

HSKL: I can possibly agree in part with that, except that I am afraid I do not understand it completely. First of all, how is it that this definition distinguishes literature from any other form of writing – say, for instance, the technical writings of scientific journals, the newspaper article, the essay, or a reporting of results in a botany experiment?

DTMR: Yes, this is the first question that comes to mind, and the answer lies in the word "involvement." The author, when he is writing literature, is relating the experiences that have involved him and the world. First, the world (or that which is exterior to him) involves the person with an experience and causes the person to undergo the experience. Then, that author's self reacts to that experience in a certain way and may produce certain feelings, emotions, thoughts, or reactions. The written relation of this experience – which is the sensing of something from the exterior to the self, or detached from the person – and the person's own interaction with the experience produces literature.

Other forms of writing do not. For example, the report of a botany experiment is only the expression of the experience; the experience being the sensing, the seeing, the hearing, of what happened in the experiment. There is not an input of one's own reactions to these. The emotions, the humor, the feelings do not enter in here. A laboratory report is strictly the recording of what happened in the experiment. It is the recording of what a person experiences in connection with the experiment firsthand and nothing else. A newspaper article is of the same genre of writing: it simply reports facts and requires no involvement from the writer except the ability to report what happened. He merely communicates what he experiences from without and then describes those immediate experiences. For example, a newspaper reporter sees an accident where two cars collide and decides to write an article on this, thinking it a newsworthy event. He immediately begins to record what has happened by means of describing what he has experienced through his eyes, nose, ears, and all the other senses through which we all experience.

HSKL: But wait a minute. If that was all there was to a lab report, then almost any kind of a scientific journal would be a list of experiences. Of course, experience is important to science because it is the raw material by which theories are composed, but I can't help but feel there is more to it. For example, if I simply say, "observe," the command is incomprehensible by itself. We need to be told what to observe or for what to look. The perception of what to observe is needed also.

DTMR: Good thought. And of course, the scientist at work in the lab will be using his mental faculties to select what to observe, and after he perceives what to observe, he observes that which is pertinent and records that in his journal.

HSKL: And so from that, I say it follows that science is literature.

DTMR: Let me finish. Although the scientist uses his various mental processes to select among all that is coming to him through the various modes by which he may observe the pertinent material for his journal, that which is recorded on his report is still not literature.

HSKL: Why?

TMR: The reason for this is that he is only writing down the experience that comes from without – i.e. the experiment or whatever he is observing – and not including any experiences that occur from within, such as those powers of reception that tell him what is relevant to the experiment. Since he does not record these experiences of the self, although they are present, this lab report is not in the realm of literature.

HSKL: I see. And the same, of course, would follow for other kinds of non-literature in that the self is not invoked in the writing.

DTMR: That's correct.

HSKL: Then how about a newspaper editorial, or an essay, or any other composition where there is not just a strict transcription of facts but, as in the case of an editorial, an opinion is incorporated into the text? Obviously, this form of exposition is more than a strict relation of facts.

DTMR: Well, Haskell, I can see by your question that according to our proposed definition of literature, we may conclude that these forms of composition have elements of the art of literature inherent in them, and I would perfectly agree. When the author adds to any piece of his written expressions of experience part of his own self, that is, some of his own interaction with that experience he is, in fact, instilling the element and basis of literature into his composition.

HSKL: Then do you believe these forms of writing should be classified and denoted as literature?

DTMR: In most cases I would not, since usually, the element of literature is small – as in the case of a newspaper editorial. But classification merely depends on your standards. If you desire to call any composition with that element of the author involving himself – expressing how he sees the world, no matter how little that may be – "literature," then it would be a valid classification as long as the standard for the classification is clearly set. Of course, as I say, these forms of writing are only rudimentary and are lesser forms of literature containing only a small interaction from the author.

HSKL: What about forms of writing where the author is wholly involving or injecting himself into his work of prose?

DTMR: Of what may you be speaking?

HSKL: What about autobiography? Is this form of writing to be considered literature or non-literature?

DTMR: If it is autobiographical in the sense that the author divorces himself from himself and writes about his life as would a biographer or a historian, then it would contain little that would lend itself to be literature. However, if the author in recording his life injected his self into his writing – that is, if he wrote of the experience of the self as well – then naturally this would become of the realm of literature.

HSKL: I see what you mean. What about other forms of writing where the author is putting his self into his work?

DTMR: Such as?

HSKL: I refer to works of philosophy such as those of Plato, Descartes, and others. Would philosophy be a form of literature or not?

DTMR: Philosophy is the process of taking assumptions drawn from the philosopher's experience and accepted as true; then to these basic assumptions he applies his thought processes in order to reach a conclusion – this is to know something more than just the original supposition assumed to be inherently valid by virtue of his experience and unequivocally true. Hence, we have the opposite case from the essay or the editorial. In philosophy the exterior experience is minimized, and the self's involvement of the writer is increased, and ideally, only the thought processes and the philosopher's logic are employed; the emotions are excluded. Hence, we can see that philosophy can certainly be defined as within the art of literature: an author takes one or more of his experiences and exerts his thoughts on these experiences in order to know something new. Consequently, he is also expressing how he sees his world. The philosopher will take any idea or thought (which is in itself an experience) and try to explain how he sees it.

HSKL: Then, when Descartes in his first "Meditation" applies thought to his experiences to understand what he knows for sure and expresses this process, he is within the realm of literature as he is doing nothing more than expressing how he sees the world.

DTMR: Exactly. When, finally, he concludes that the only thing he knows for sure is that he thinks, he has expressed that the only experience that he can understand and know for sure is that he thinks – he establishes that as a basic assumption, and proceeds to apply the faculties of his self, and we can follow him as he describes how he sees his world in those six most brilliant meditations.

HSKL: Yes, I can see now that philosophy is but a form of literature if we accept that original definition of the art of literature. As for Descartes or any other philosopher, he does indeed employ the experience of thought to express how he sees the world. However, I have another question regarding what is and is not literature.

DTMR: Please, by all means.

HSKL: What about something that deals in abstractions such as a mathematics dissertation?

DTMR: Well, of course, if we speak of a text, then that has no relation to literature since it is just a compilation of other documents. However, if you speak of an original manuscript where we can see a mathematician apply his thought processes to a certain set of assumptions and can see and follow his thought (and, of course, this thought is being actually experienced by the mathematician himself), then we have the elements of literature present – those constituents being the assumptions and the application of logic. The assumptions derive themselves, however divorced and distant they may seem from the original experience being designated by symbols, from certain basic abstractions of experience. Thus, we may say that all mathematics derives itself from experience.

Let us take the simplest of examples. The idea of the number "one." If a person sees a cow, he thereby experiences the sight and then the thought of one cow. He then abstracts this idea of "one" into the symbol of "1." The same is done with two cows as the idea of "two" is expressed with the symbol "2." A man can then symbolize the cow and the idea of "1" together by making it 1x or in the case of two cows, 2x. If he sees this one cow (1x), and standing separately from this he notices two other cows in the same field, he might come to the conclusion that there are three cows in the field, and express it in a rather distant and divorced manner by symbolizing the situation as $1x + 2x = 3x$. Now, this may sound a bit childish, Haskell – even though the world of mathematics is profound and at first sight, the most complicated of mathematics appears to have no relation to experience – but one can find in any case a route from the most complex of expressions back to some root in simple experience however distant the road is.

HSKL: So, the mathematician's abstractions have a basis in experience, and the expression of his thought processes about these divorced symbols of experience can be construed as a form of literature. Like the philosopher, he is expressing a view of the world – however distant it may seem.

DTMR: Yes. If we can watch his thought process and see how he thinks, then the written expression of this would have the basic components of what is to be called literature.

HSKL: I can begin to see your point. The art of literature is the expression of how the author sees the world through his experiences, and I can see how we might understand a mathematical monograph to be of the realm of literature. I have often heard the phrases "mathematical literature" and the "the art of mathematics" used. However, whether all mathematics is rooted in experience I am not so sure. So, I'm still a bit unsure as to whether our definition of literature is completely valid, or whether mathematics is truly of the realm of the art of literature. Let me ask you still about the symbols of the mathematician and their having a basis in experience.

DTMR: Please do. I feel, proceeding in this line of questioning, we are going to come upon something that is quite worthwhile to pursue and may prove valuable at a later time. Please proceed.

HSKL: Thank you. What about symbols such as those representing imaginary numbers, or how about the symbol of negative time which often appears in the study of physics? These symbols have no antecedents in the real world as far as we can realize or experience.

DTMR: Haskell, please remember what mathematicians do along with philosophers. They take suppositions, apply logic and other thought processes, and form a conclusion. Often in this process new symbols such as the ones you mentioned appear, but they are only symbols that represent a situation that might possibly exist, but of which we have no experience. Hence, we cannot conceive in our minds how the situation of, say, negative time could exist in this world, as we have experienced nothing that would enable us to conceive of such a situation ever presenting itself to us in our world as we presently experience it. Of course, in the process of mathematics, symbols are manifested that have no probable antecedents in the world, but the unreal situations which these symbols suggest cannot possibly be spontaneously realized by the mathematician (or anybody else) without a prior experience that would lend itself to the discovery of the symbol and the suggestion that such a situation may exist and possibly even be experienced.

HSKL: Well, what about the thought of negative time? People have been thinking and writing of this concept, you must admit, for who knows how long, and yet this has no clear basis in the real world.

DTMR: Absolutely true. People have had that thought for some time with no previous experience of it. However, since the mathematician/physicist's symbol of negative time arose from the process of applying logic to supposition, postulation, theorem, etc., the mathematician/physicist may only say that given these assumptions this situation may arise if we extend our experience farther – but then again, it might not. The mathematician/physicist can only predict that there is a mathematical feasibility, but this mathematical situation may extend farther than the real world. It certainly extends farther than our present experience of the real world. Hence, we cannot really know the concept in question. We cannot realize its meaning fully because we have no experience of it, as in this example of negative time. This symbol manifested itself with the advance of modern physics, giving the physicist the idea that there exists a mathematical basis of negative time – and hence the possibility of its existence! However, because a person has not yet had any experience with negative time, he cannot possibly completely know it in his mind. That is, the possibility of it existing in our world is incredible and unimaginable because of our limited experience.

Now, getting back to the original point of all this, when people write stories of time machines going back into history, or think of other fantastic ideas that occur in science fiction literature, these ideas are produced by ordinary experiences that we have already experienced. For example, we have experienced that most things on this earth that move can move forward and backward. Plus, we already have the experience of frequently taking one idea that we know, extrapolating it, and applying it to another. Consequently, a person may take the idea of forward and backward motion, which has been experienced, and apply it to time, which we know and think of as a forward process. Hence, the idea of negative time arises. But we must be careful here. We know the idea in a limited sense only: the motions of forward and backward are known (because of our having experienced it) and the idea behind the words "negative time" is known (because of our having experienced the idea behind the words), but not negative time itself. That is, we cannot know the concept of negative time, but only the term and the superficial idea.

I must insist, Haskell, that neither you nor anybody else can know negative time and feel all the consequences of it (should it exist) if you have not experienced it. We cannot, as we have never had any experience in that direction, know fully and completely for what the symbol of negative time or any other like symbol stands.

HSKL: Then I perceive from what you have said that any idea that comes to mind cannot be completely known and written about if we have not experienced that idea; and thus, any new thought that springs spontaneously to our mind as a result of the intermixing of our experiences and our thought processes cannot be strictly known if it itself is not an experience. I am now wondering, Detmar, what is the nature of the idea, and how is it that one cannot know a certain idea even though it has sprung from the person's very self? It has come from a person and yet he cannot know it!

DTMR: That is correct, Haskell. Now, let us consider the nature of an idea. When something that has been realized or known is given thought or is applied by the brain, something may occur that is new and novel. For instance, let us use our example of negative time. We experience and know time. We also have experienced the motions of forward and backward. Then with one or more of the various processes of the mind, one can extrapolate by applying the experience of backwardness to that of time; hence, the idea of negative time is revealed. But of course, we cannot fully realize negative time because we have not experienced it. Let me take another example. Suppose, as you mentioned once, you have never been to Paris, but through your experiences of reading books and hearing people talk who have been to Paris, you have a partial conception of Paris which is perfectly known as far as the conception itself is an experience. To this conception, you add, by a process of the mind, the known experience of traveling. The result is the idea of going to Paris and there acquiring the opportunity of seeing Paris firsthand. Now, you must admit that your idea of Paris is known only as far as you have read and heard of it, and since those actions were experienced, the idea of Paris, as developed as it is, is perfectly known to that extent that it has been acquired by experience. But when you add the process of thought that gives rise to the idea of going to and being in Paris and seeing yourself before the Louvre, every integral part of that picture in your mind has been made available only by actual experience plus thought processes (which are also experiences).

Any new addition can only be added by the acquisition of a new experience. And so, to acquire a perfect idea of standing in front of the Louvre, you, Haskell, will have to go to Paris and stand in front of the Louvre.

To further the example, take the case of a famous mathematician whose equations, based on reality, extend past worldly experience and produce a new idea – like that of going to Paris – that is not known yet in that it has not been experienced. Like the extrapolation of your experiences to the situation of standing in front of the Louvre, the mathematician extends his equations to a situation not yet discovered by experience, and the new idea takes on the role of a prediction. We must remember that prediction is not known completely until we have experienced it, just as we cannot know what it is like to be in front of the Louvre until we have been there, but we can predict what it will be like on the basis of what we do know or have experienced concerning that subject.

HSKL: Yes, I now can understand the meaning of an idea. But what do you mean by these words you continually repeat, namely, "thought processes?"

DTMR: As you well know, the mind is capable of operating logically, and each person has certain abilities and certain deficiencies when coming up against the various problems that occur throughout life. If we take notice of these, we can immediately see examples of "thought" or "thought processes." For instance, children vary in their ability to put together a puzzle; some children are just faster than others in being able to use one facet of their cerebral faculties. Another child, who cannot piece puzzles together as quickly as his neighbor, may very well be able to read a map with great ability and be able to recognize the directions, symbols, distances, etc., and understand all the intricacies of them much more easily than the child who was so adroit with the puzzle. Hence, if we notice the differences in the way people think and perceive things, then when I say "thought process" one can see that I simply refer to the use of inductive and deductive logic, recall, association, etc., in their applications to different situations.

HSKL: I see. I'm sorry I have taken us so far off the track, but I thought it important to clear up some points in my mind before we proceeded. Then, recalling the mathematician who writes a dissertation and explains within it how he has thought and shown his process of thinking (which is itself an experience), he is expressing his experiences (which in his case can be almost the same – that is, his experiences can be his thoughts) and therefore, he has the essence of literature within the dissertation. I believe that is what we came to before we diverted our attention to the nature of ideas.

DTMR: That is correct. A mathematical dissertation can have the essential elements of literature. But Haskell, what may be called a great mathematical dissertation, or what may be called a great piece of philosophy, or a great essay may not necessarily be thought of as an outstanding piece of literature, and of course, vice versa. It is just that we must keep in mind what the basis of the art of literature is, and thereby we may be able to recognize what forms of writing begin to become literature.

HSKL: I see. But now, Detmar, you have raised another question in my mind.

DTMR: Yes?

HSKL: What would great literature be, or how is it that one may be able to recognize and determine quality in the art of literature?

DTMR: Ah, an interesting question, Haskell. Suppose we take our proposed definition of literature (the written representation of how one sees the world, or how one has experienced and interacted with the world) and apply it as a yardstick for purposes of criticism. Would you not think that would be the first step to determine whether a piece of literature is of quality or not?

HSKL: Yes, it certainly sounds like the first step to me; however, I am not at all clear what would be the method of application of our proposed definition, and how we could critically view literature with this in mind.

DTMR: Well, when we examine an author's words, we must judge whether the author has truly, faithfully, and precisely related how he sees the world. He must come as close as possible to depicting just how he has experienced and just how he has interacted with these experiences. And, he must be consistent with these experiences.

HSKL: Can that be so, Detmar? I can hardly believe you are telling me this. Please excuse my vehement reaction, but surely you cannot be serious. Can you possibly think that all the things an author writes are his forthright descriptions of how he sees the world, or how he has experienced the world and his interactions with it? Let me take any author as an instance, and you will have to reconsider. For example, the contents of the novels of Charles Dickens do not relate precisely to the author's life. Of course, I can see similarities and parallels to the events of his life to those that he depicted so beautifully in his great works of literature. But Charles Dickens is perhaps the most mild of examples that come to mind, as there is that strong correspondence of events between his novels and real life. However, the fact remains that the things the novels do relate, and the incidents of his real life are quite different. Dickens did not live his life exactly as is described in his works of art.

Better examples would be Kafka, Ambrose Bierce, or Poe, whose out-of-the-ordinary stories certainly could not have been experienced by the authors just as they relate in their stories. But really any author will do; none of them ever expresses anything exactly as it occurred in his life. How is it that we could possibly account for this discrepancy by using this view of literature? Clearly, there is something lacking in our definition, or else we have gone astray.

DTMR: Indeed. I see your concern. First, let us remember our definition of literature, which was how the author sees the world – or in more explicit terms, the written expression of how the author's internal experiences interact with his external experiences. It is this addition of the emotions, thoughts, feelings, etc., of the self to those external experiences that are seen, heard, or in some other way sensed and received by the self that instills the quality of literature in an exposition.

Hence, when an author sets himself before the pen and paper, his self becomes totally involved in what is to be written and he is not bound at any length to report the realities (that is, just what happened) of those external experiences if he wishes not to do so. His only obligation is to be true and faithful to how he sees the world, and in what terms he depicts this does not matter. As long as he is accurately, faithfully, and truly describing his interactions or his internal experiences with his external experiences, or how the writer views that world, then he is fulfilling his obligations as an author of literature.

HSKL: But why does he change the actual events of his life into some other sets of events, circumstances, and situations in some cases so divorced from his own life that it seems he would hardly have ever experienced anything even closely related to the contents of his story?

DTMR: Well, Haskell, neither you nor I nor anybody else can tell any certain individual's needs, likings, dislikings, mental problems, physical problems, or anything else connected with that person's self without some indication from him. I cannot tell you in any particular case the specific motives why anyone author does so; I can say that these needs, preferences, problems, etc., cause him to choose circumstances for his writing that are indirect to his life. The human being is complex. Suppose an author is embarrassed to relate any direct reference to his experiences concerning his mother and father. If this hampers and hinders the portrayal of how he views his life and experiences surrounding those concerned with his parents, he will choose a different or indirect medium to relate his story. In order to enable himself to limn the situation faithfully he will cloak it in indirect and divorced circumstances alleviating him of the burden of embarrassment that may weigh heavily upon him.

There are an indefinite number of reasons an author may have for selecting a specific path of expression. Again, Haskell, he may see a certain person who is thought honorable and just by all those around – except by the writer, who sees this person in terms of a clown or a scoundrel. In his written representation of the experience he may want to delineate himself in terms of a buffoon and reveal that character by his total set of internal and external experiences. That is, he views this man as a base being, and if he represents faithfully and completely just how that man appears to him, then it becomes what we should call good literature.

HSKL: I'm beginning to understand what you are explaining: that we cannot know why an author will select a certain way or a certain set of circumstances for the characters or why the author will even select certain characters. Indeed, we cannot know any motive concerning why the author chooses what he does in order to convey a certain set of experiences that are within him. Even if, say, a character whom he describes in a story has never appeared with that name or appearance before in the author's life, that character can be invented because the author has experienced enough of the world to make a composite of those people he has actually met. Without this prior experience of the actual world, he could not make this composite character of which he writes. Everything in the character, every gesture, every thought, every action, comes from the author's experience of the world. Perhaps, they are all experiences from the author's life, and they are either experiences that originate from within oneself or from without.

DTMR: Haskell, you are not just beginning to understand this concept of literature; you seem to fully understand it.

HSKL: Thank you, but as of yet there are still many points about which I am left in the dark. When people say the imagination of an author is wonderful or great, they speak of something that truly seems to be. It seems that an author must have a good imagination in order to write novels, short stories, plays, or whatever. This term "imagination" seems to be incongruous with what we have established: that the entire contents of written expression are drawn from experience and thus, can be said to be entirely of memory. What about imagination and literature? Is it possible to reconcile the author's use of his imagination and our concept of literature?

DTMR: Yes, I would think that we may be able to do so. You have said yourself that the contents of a piece of literature may not be directly taken from the author's life, yet all the events that are written and depicted in the story are extracts from the artist's experience, and that which is expressed in the piece of literary art becomes a composite of sorts. Also, when we were discussing the notion of experience itself, we noted that one of the ways of thought in which some people are proficient is the method of combining two known experiences (the experience of time and the experience of backward motion) and contemplating the result. If an author takes a character whom he knows and introduces him to another character, he introduces a new set of circumstances (the constituents of which are known and have been experienced), and then the author draws upon his faculties again to give him the power of expression to portray through his experiences the result of such a meeting. The result of such a meeting of the characters is still taken from what is known to the author in that the author describes what would happen on such an occasion and it is his experience that such a result would happen. How much is known of the result directly depends on the amount of experience in that vein. Possibly, as in the case of negative time, very little will be known, or possibly the result will already have been experienced and fully known. The author in the case of his two characters knows a great deal. Consequently, the imagination of the author lies in his ability to draw up and combine various experiences for the sake of his tale.

HSKL: I see. I would now like to venture to presume that literature such as allegories, which seem to border on fantasies, is based on the author's experience, but how can these fantasies be based in the author's experience?

DTMR: Well again, taking our perspective of literature, we must search for the way the allegory is rooted in experience, which it must certainly be if it is literature at all. But, what is interesting here is the fact that the author of an allegory places a distance between himself and his experiences, and indeed seems to dwell in fantasy that deviates much and far from human experience. Again, we may not be able to know for certain why an author chooses such a medium as an allegory to express how he sees the world; his reasons and motives may be many and varied. For example, if the author wants to satirize somebody or something, but lives under an oppressive political government in which, if he forthrightly satirizes some dangerous subject, he may become subject to a punishment of some kind. Consequently, in order to prevent this he may dull or distance the irony of his exposition by relating it symbolically in distant and obscure terms; but nevertheless, it is rooted in his experience, and its foundation is in his view of the world. Of course, there is a myriad of other examples of why he may choose not to relate directly his own personal experience but prefer to disguise them in different circumstances about which we have already hinted previously. But we must not forget that in good literature, even though the terms in which the author describes his experiences may be ever so obscure, they are actually describing how the author sees the world.

HSKL: Then, again, you contend that the allegory is no different from other forms of literature that are not so symbolic and so distant from the author's experiences and knowledge of the world.   It is only this degree of distance and obscurity in symbolism that makes the allegory. Its roots are, nevertheless, planted in the writer's view of the world.

DTMR: That is absolutely right, and what you just mentioned is the key to understanding the allegory or any other form of literature. That is, the author sees the world in the terms in which he writes.   If he chooses to write an obscurely symbolic delineation of the world, it is only because he sees his experiences in this way.   What I mentioned a little bit ago concerning someone writing under an oppressive government – or any other reason why an author chooses the terms he does – is all secondary and inconsequential. I put forth those examples only as possible reasons that may work upon an author's mind; but, of course, what I have wanted to purport all along is the fact that no matter what form of expression is chosen, the main concern of the artist is to relate as fully and exactly as possible just how he, the author, sees the world.

HSKL: I see the point entirely now.

DTMR: But let me continue a bit. We are now at a crucial stage in understanding the nature of literature.   When an author describes his experiences of how he sees the world, he invariably uses simile and metaphor. That is, he will say, "I understand my circumstances in this light or in these terms and this is how it looks to me." He will declare that one thing is like another or that one thing is another. To be sure, he believes, and it is his experience, that he sees those things in terms of something else. Or he will state "I believe through my experiences that I see things in terms of those things." And this, Haskell, my friend, is what gives value to literature, and it is the reason why we place great importance on literature, and on all of art itself.

But let me return to metaphor and simile. These devices appear at two levels in art. The first is where the author applies them within his story by expressing that one thing is or is like another because he sees it as such. The second level is that his whole work may be said to be an expression that is or is like his life. Indeed, any piece of literature is such – the expression of the author exclaiming that his experiences are seen in these certain terms. Hence, he will say, he views the world in this manner and his literature is or is like his life. That is, one thing is or is like another.

HSKL: I believe now I have come to a fuller understanding of literature. But what is this you mention about the value of literature? Could you elaborate on that point, as I am not sure I understand yet where the value of literature lies?

DTMR: Yes. The value of literature lies simply in the fact that we are allowed to see another man's perception of the world and the difference of his experiences. There, in the difference in how he perceives his experiences, lies the value of literary art (or for that matter any kind of art). If his experiences are different, then we may value the opportunity to consider these new experiences by enjoying the expression of them by someone who has undergone events not yet experienced by us. If we have undergone the experience or one similar to it (so that we may know most of it yet may not know it completely), we may thereby observe the difference in how the author interacts and regards the experience. Again, we may benefit from and enjoy the description of that difference.

HSKL: Well, Detmar, I have no questions following our present line of thought. However, I would like to return to the point which gave rise to the most recent part of our disquisition, what good literature is, and continue again from there. If I recall correctly, you asserted that the criterion on which one should use to approach literature is the determination of the truthfulness, precision, faithfulness, consistency, and completeness of the author's work.

DTMR: Yes. Those are factors that determine the quality of any given piece of literature. But in criticizing, judging, or examining a work of literature, we are, Haskell, taking these factors – which, by the way, are determinants in judging most anything – and applying them to a standard of some sort in this case involving the author's written delineation of his experiences.

HSKL: This is essentially how my professors criticize and examine not only the writings of great authors but also the papers we students submit to them.

DTMR: And they are correct, I would think, in their method of application. Is it not obvious that any written expression must have consistency, clarity, exactness, in what the writer has to say?

HSKL: Yes, without a doubt.

DTMR: And in order to gain a complete assessment of something, it would be better, in my mind at least, to know the essence and nature of what it is you are evaluating. Would you not agree?

HSKL: Yes. If I understand you, you say that these factors of faithfulness, clarity, accuracy, consistency, etc., when applied to written expression, are the means to obtain an evaluation of the expression; but to acquire a more complete assessment of what one is critiquing, one must understand the essence of what one is critiquing or evaluating.

DTMR: That is essentially my stand on the subject.

HSKL: There are but two more questions I have on the nature of literature and how to approach it.

DTMR: Please let me hear them.

HSKL: The first query arises from my curiosity as to just how you apply these determinants of quality to any particular subject, and, specifically, literature. That is, just how can we determine what good literature is using the measurements of accuracy, faithfulness, consistency, etc., upon the author's work, keeping in mind that literature is the description of how the author views his experiences? One of the circumstances that contributed to the rise of this question of how to judge literature was occasioned by my recently perusing a sample of modern poetry and noticing a significant amount of obscurity prevalent. Perhaps the problem is my lack of perception and intelligence, or perhaps some of the poetry that I have read of late is not of a high quality. But wherever the fault may lie, the problem of not being able to surmise to any extent whether the poetry which I have read has great or little value, or indeed should be considered good poetry or bad, is of pressing importance in my mind. I do not necessarily judge as a matter of course what I read, as I usually read for the sheer pleasure of it, and if I find it fun or interesting or in some way pleasant, I naturally, without thinking very profoundly about it, consider it basically a good book. However, if the book of prose or verse was not pleasant in reading, I sometimes wonder if it has good value and if it is a good piece of literature at all.

Also, as happens to everyone at one time or another, we are confronted with the question of who is the best author, or is this author better than that; or when it comes to contemporary authors, the question is whether this or that author is any good. It is at these times that I am quite at a loss, as I have no specific system in mind to realize a reasonable judgment and be able to make a critical evaluation of a work of literature. I simply fall back to the simple, subjective standard of whether or not I like it.

DTMR: Well, I believe we have all the necessary ingredients before us that are needed to be able to approach a work of prose or verse to view it in a proper light, although I am not sure we are going to be able to settle some of these questions such as which author is better than another. But I believe we will be able to establish a way to approach literature so that we can be able to make criticisms and judgments as to the quality of the work, for as we well know, art is not above criticism. Indeed it is obvious that some works are better than others, and some are poor while some are great, with all levels of quality in between.

HSKL: Yes, Detmar, most anyone would agree with that.

DTMR: If we have before us a task requiring our criticism of a work of literature, then the first thing we must do is to fix in our minds our definition of literature. Then as we read, we must pose to ourselves whether or not the materials we are reading fulfill our definition; that is, is the author relating how he sees his circumstances and expressing the interaction between himself and that which is apart from himself? Next, taking this definition, we should decide how well he is succeeding, and it is here we employ the concepts of faithfulness, consistency, completeness, and other similar notions. For example, we must scrutinize whether the author is faithfully and consistently relating his experiences as he sees them: he should transcribe without deviation how he perceives his experiences of the world; obviously, he must tell his story completely since surely incompleteness cannot be tolerated; and he should be exact as possible in describing his tale. There may be other notions that are the same or similar to these just mentioned that should or should not be included here as necessary for judgment; however, they are not so important, as they are all obvious requirements that any criticism would employ in its examination of not only any piece of writing but any work of literature or art – or indeed, anything else where evaluation is possible.

Furthermore, these notions mentioned are not just to be used for criticism of art but may be used where any standard exists. A standard is not necessarily limited to the definition of literature or to a definition of art or to one of music, but to anything where there is an essence or where an essence can be discerned and understood.

HSKL: I'm not sure I completely follow you.

DTMR: Do you understand what I mean by the term "standard"?

HSKL: Not completely.

DTMR: It simply means a knowledge of an essence or a nature. Suppose a critic is going to evaluate two works of prose literature. The contents of each are different; however, there is that essence or nature that is common in both in which we realize the idea (or essence) of the art of literature. Moreover, common natures are not only found in literature. We may also possibly discover standards, or their essences, by which to know art, beauty, philosophy, liberty, justice, truth, or any idea or notion that may come into our head. Even simpler ideas have a basic essence, and indeed all words themselves have an idea or notion behind them, and they can be defined; hence the essence can be realized and comprehended. And Haskell, do not forget that all these ideas, and words themselves, have their origins in experiences. It is our experience that incorporates and instills these ideas into our brain. Take any word, however abstract or concrete its meaning may be, we may trace its origin to experience.

HSKL: Yes, I now can understand that fully. But I wonder if you would give an example of applying the notions of general criticism to literature or art in general.

DTMR: Fine. But let us leave art in general for later and for now limit our discourse to the present topic, literature. In applying the notions of judgment to literature, we have said that these concepts are utilized to judge anything that has a standard – that is, anything that can be defined like, for example, a game that we might play. A game has a set of rules, and consequently is ordered in a certain fashion, and when we consider whether or not the game is a good one, we make judgments on whether it is fun and interesting. However, upon venturing to make a bit more profound appraisal of the game, we must proceed past our superficial first impressions and consider the rules (as the rules are the essence of a game and a game is but the rules) by putting to task our aforementioned conceptions. Hence, naturally, we would deliberate whether or not the rules are consistent, hold no contradictions, and are complete and entire. If the rules hold these characteristics, we would be able to judge them as suitable and good. If the rules are not consistent, have contradictions, or are not complete, then they cannot be completely suitable and good. Consequently, when the game is experienced, it surely will not be as interesting, as enjoyable, as much fun, as it would be if it were completely consistent.

Next, once the rules are established, suitable, and good, and once we know the rules (which are the essence of the game), we may then determine how to play the game and may come to realize how to judge and criticize the game like any referee. But of course, in order to become a competent referee one must know (and therefore experience) the standard by which he is to judge. In other words, he must know completely the essence of the game. Would you not say so, Haskell?

HSKL: Indeed, I would. But the judging and criticizing of a game are surely different from the judging and critiquing of a novel or a poem, I would imagine.

DTMR: Haskell, think a bit. They are exactly the same. Let me say again that we will apply these notions to anything with an essence or a certain nature about it. The essence of a game is its rules; the essence of a government (ideally speaking) is its constitution and its laws, and thus, any law or any constitution or indeed any exposition may be critiqued by the notions of consistency, completeness, congruity, and all other such ideas of which one might be able to think. This seems to me to be common sense and obvious.

Now, let us proceed to literature. Since there is certainly an essence in literature (which we have captured and been able to define), we are free to apply the ideas and notions that are to be employed by criticism and applied to a work of literature to determine its quality. We inquire whether or not the contents of the novel or poem are consistent, congruous, entire, and complete, and hold no contradictions. It is at this point we need to know the essence of the thing we judge – that is, we need to have the standard by which we can consider the congruity, the consistency of the thing we will assess. We must be able to establish to what the thing (in this case, the work of literature) is consistent and congruent. In the case of the game, we had the rules which provided the reference or standard which could be exercised. In literature, we have the attainment and realization of the essence (which is our definition), and hence, we can have that standard by which to judge. Our procedure does not vary from that of the game: we observe the action of the game and notice if it is consistent, congruent, and in accordance with the rules of the game. In literature, we observe the written expression of the work of art and notice if it is consistent, without contradiction, congruent, and in accordance with the essence of literature.

HSKL: The method is now clear and lucid in my mind thanks to your explanation, Detmar. But how can we know if the contents of the prose or verse have all these things you say they must have? For instance, how can we know if an author's expression has consistency and congruity, and fullness? I understand that we are to examine the contents of a work in light of our definition (how the author sees his experiences) and consider if the contents are consistent with the standard. But I cannot quite grasp yet how we could manage this. Could you explain to me the process that would enable me to go about making a correct approach to criticism of literature? What kind of things should we look for when employing this method?

DTMR: Well, Haskell, remembering that literature is the written expression of how the author experiences his world, we can soon realize the most important point to look for, and that would be whether the author is relating things true to his experience. Is he consistent and congruent in his representation; does he delineate his experience fully, completely, and truly as he has experienced them; and are there any contradictions within the story? These are the questions we must employ.

HSKL: Then how do we know when the author goes amiss in his depiction of his experiences? Certainly, it must be fairly difficult to discern any deviation, since usually, the author has already cloaked his experiences in a setting different from the original in order to facilitate expression of how he perceives his world.

DTMR: There are two ways. First, we must utilize our own experiences, which tell us whether the author's representations are consistent, etc. For instance, we might take a character of a novel and look upon him in light of our own experiences and ask: could such a character as this say such things; would he perform such actions; might he say or think, for instance, such evil or joyful things or whatever? The point is that because we are human individuals similar to the author and have experienced many similar things, we can know many of the same things the author does, and consequently can know whether his depictions are truthful and faithful to his experiences.

HSKL: What is the second way?

DTMR: The second way must be employed when we do not have similar experiences that correspond to that of the author's, which must invariably happen as we are different individuals in different places and in different times. Hence, obviously, our experiences must vary. Consequently, we cannot know entirely what the author knows. In such a case we must test the relation of the story just by whether it is consistent within itself (that is, there are no contradictions and it is congruent), and if it is consistent by comparison to other people's experiences and/or written representations of similar experiences.

HSKL: Thank you, Detmar. This matter is completely clear in my mind. But there are a few more questions that have come to mind that were touched upon before but I did not have a chance to pursue fully. Thus, at this point I would like to ask about one of the various forms of fiction and whether it is a valid form of literature, whether the same criteria by which we define and judge other literature can also be applied.

DTMR: And what's that?

HSKL: Science fiction. Is it really literature, and can the extraordinary ideas and fantasies of this genre be considered as how the author sees his world?

DTMR: I will answer "yes" to both parts of that question.

HSKL: Then I wonder if you could elaborate on that so I might be able to understand how it is.

DTMR: Well, first, in order to establish whether it is literature or not, we must decide if the author expresses himself in the way he sees and perceives his total set of experiences – those originating from without, those that originate from within, and those interacting with those from without.

HSKL: Yes, I can follow that. If I may reiterate what we have already established, the written expression that includes only those experiences originating from without, such as seeing something or hearing something, is only of the level of the newspaper article or the laboratory report. And that expression which adds the experiences that originate from within oneself and/or interact with those from without, such as fear, anger, happiness, depression, meditation, pure thought, can be classified in the category of literature. Now, I believe only from this point can we establish if science fiction is of the realm of literature.

DTMR: Yes. There is only one basic difference that distinguishes science fiction from the rest of literature. This is the addition of an idea that is not wholly known by experience, and this is used as a supposition in order to enable the author to expand upon a set of experiences that he might not otherwise have the chance to depict. This supposition (or these suppositions) derives itself from the author's experience but is not yet completely known through experience. For example, suppose a writer of science fiction literature has experienced through his education that there is a probability that other forms of life may be existent somewhere within the universe and man is not alone. The processes of his mind then proceed to construct how there could be a form of life that inhabits, for example, space, through the use of what he already knows (through his experiences) and by letting the mind extrapolate these to form a possibility of what the creature would be like and what it would be like to encounter one in a given set of circumstances. The author will want to give vent to his thoughts. Hence, he will express how he sees his experiences if these or those circumstances were to be. Thus, the basic difference is the addition of a supposition or suppositions to the story – usually concerning the future, though it can concern the past also if the author is so disposed. But in either case, it is the input of an idea that has not yet been fully experienced, albeit its other components have.

HSKL: I see. But I wondered where this idea comes from and how it occurs to the author if he has not, as you say, fully experienced it.

DTMR: If you will remember, I believe we touched upon this process before, but if you wish we can examine once more where ideas come from. Taking the case of our science fiction writer, he may want to write about how he believes there might be life existing in space, and how it might act if it were to come into contact with us earthlings and vice versa. First, the author has a certain set of experiences that has taught him about the needs of life and much about its workings – although, of course, not everything has been discovered yet. Thus, he knows about life's needs and processes, and he also knows some things about space. At this point, the mind in its processes can combine the knowledge of two experiences to produce the idea of something that might be experienced, and at this point, the mind has come to predict something. In science fiction, the author writes how he sees these predictions. He may extrapolate how life may exist in space and express what it may do and so on.

HSKL: There is something called "fantasy science fiction" that I am wondering about. Is this also a form of the art of literature?

DTMR: The art of science fiction literature is the expression of how the author sees the world suppositionally; however, we must remember that expression of experience is still the basis of literature, and indeed of all art, and the more you deviate from this, the more the value of the art of literature will decrease. Consequently, if in a science fiction novel, the basis of experience is forgotten and it deals with illogical, unpredictable, and impossible events throughout, then its artistic and literary value disappears and all that remains is escapism with no greater value than that of simple entertainment.

However, a science fiction novel may use an assumption or speculation that may be highly fantastical in conception and may have its basis in distant experience, if a purpose exists to show by experience what would happen in a given set of circumstances; that is, an author may want to probe a certain set of human experiences, but in order to discuss them a rather fantastical predicament or presupposition far from the reaches of experience is needed. Then an author may be allowed to employ these extravagant suppositions as long as what proceeds is steeped in his experience so that the quality of literature can be perceived and appreciated.

HSKL: I believe at this point I am completely satisfied in respect to my uncertainties concerning our definition of literature. Now, I would like to ask you about something you have been saying throughout this entire discourse, and that is the phrase, "the art of literature." I would like to inquire, when we defined "literature," if we still could have retained the same definition if we had extended "literature" to be the "art of literature." I certainly feel that all literature is within the realm of art, but it has occurred to me that if our definition of literature is the definition of the art of literature, then within that circumscription we may be able to locate the essence of art – and possibly of aesthetics also.

DTMR: Your sagacity is impressive.

HSKL: Thank you, Detmar. But may I ask if you have some thoughts on the essence and nature of all art?

DTMR: Haskell, unfortunately, it is becoming late and this would be a good point to take a break until tomorrow before we start a discussion on the nature of art.

HSKL: What time will you be free?

DTMR: Anytime after lunch.

HSKL: Thank you. I shall be sure to come by, Detmar.

DTMR: I'll be expecting you. Good day!

THE NATURE OF ART

DTMR: Come in, Haskell! Good to see you. How are you today?

HSKL: Fine, thanks. And I'm most anxious to resume our discussion of yesterday as I have given the subject some thought since then.

DTMR: Haskell, you of course know there is nothing that I like more than to examine with you these most fascinating subjects in which you are so interested.

HSKL: I'm glad to hear that as I take up a great deal of your time.

DTMR: Not at all.

HSKL: Well then, let me get right to the point where we left off yesterday. I am now completely satisfied with our definition of literature, but you raised a point that I have not been able to resolve or clarify in my mind. This pertains to mixing the expressions "the definition of literature" and "the definition of the art of literature." I, of course, believe that literature is a part of art, but in what way, I have not been able to determine. I was wondering if you could resolve that point for me; and also, if I am not asking too much, I was wondering if we could now pursue what art itself is.

DTMR: Alright, but since we have established already what the nature of literature is, I believe we may soon readily ascertain the essence of art and the relation between the two, since, as you have already surmised, they are indeed very close.

HSKL: Then you might be able to offer a proposal of its nature?

DTMR: Let us commence by putting forth the proposition that art is the expression of how the artist sees his total set of experiences.

HSKL: You were not jesting when you said that the postulation for the art of literature was close to that of art itself. In fact, it is so close I am having difficulty deeming how it is that they differ, except that I can remember that you often used the additional words "written expression" when referring to literature.

DTMR: Yes, that is correct. It stands to reason that if literature is a form of art, the definition of art had better be more encompassing than that of literature, since we have supposed that all literature is a form of art.

HSKL: Yes, there will be no argument from me upon that point. However, does this propositional definition encompass all the various forms of art and can we readily be able to denote the type of art with a proper definition of its nature?

DTMR: As I think you can already see, this definition proposal is inclusive of all forms of art, and with each form, we must simply describe in which manner and medium the particular mode of art expresses itself. Let us take, for example, what is commonly called art – or in other words, painting pictures. We may, I believe, readily assign it to be the visual representation on canvas of the way the artist sees his experiences. Taking another instance, we could say that sculpture is the three-dimensional depiction of the way the artist sees the world; thus, one who expresses himself in the medium of three dimensions would be denoted an artist of sculpture.

HSKL: Let me see if I understand you correctly. During all that time yesterday when we were endeavoring to establish an understanding of the nature of literature, we were, in fact, moving toward a grasping of the concept of art in general, except that we were using restrictive terms which kept the subject matter confined to the art of literature only. Also, when I agreed to our definition of literature and came to realize it completely, I had in effect come to understand the nature of all art.

DTMR: It would appear so.

HSKL: Then. I wonder if we could possibly take a step or two backward since it would help me with a problem or two as this new sudden comprehension of mine has evidently not completely settled and solidified in my mind. Even though I should be fully convinced and should fully understand our newly proposed definition of art in total, could you possibly again explain to me the essence of art?

DTMR: First, let us get our terms straight. Hereafter, when we speak of art, we will mean all that is in the realm of art and not just the painting of pictures – which let us call "painting." Now, let us go over our proposed definition of art which we essentially derived and examined yesterday.

HSKL: Thank you.

DTMR: Art is the expression of how the artist sees his total set of experiences. An artist takes it upon himself to depict through a medium that most facilitates his expression the terms by which he sees the world. The basic material is, of course, experience. The artist has experiences originating from within and from without his person. These inner experiences such as his feelings, anger, emotions, and thought processes all interact (except possibly deep meditation) with those originating in the exterior and constitute the author's complete set of experiences. It is the author's consideration and then the expression of this constitution of experiences that are the essence and process of art. Let me give again the example of painting. Here the processes of the artist's mind tend to operate in a rather visual capacity; hence, when he chooses to express how he realizes his world, he chooses to express himself naturally in the manner which would most easily facilitate his expression to its optimum, and since the makeup of his mind seems to operate in a visual capacity as opposed to that of a verbal one, he will give vent to his own particular world and the experiences which make up that world through painting.

HSKL: Again, I hesitate to agree with you completely. When I look upon some of the art today and see how abstract it is and how unrelated it seems to me to be from one's experiences, I cannot help but think that the artist must be relating or describing something else besides his experiences. Also, when I take in some abstract art, it seems so different and divorced from anything in my experience that it completely befuddles and confounds me to the extent that I wonder if the subject of the art could have been experienced by anyone at all. Any one of numerous examples of modern sculpture or painting or even the new art of photography will serve as an instance of what I mean.

DTMR: I can understand the problem, but we can apply the same principles of literature that we came to understand yesterday to this problem of obscurity in modern art that faces us today.

HSKL: I hope so. I would like to come to a complete understanding of the nature of art.

DTMR: First, let us not deal with that which is so abstract and obscure, as are some of the modern artists, but let us take an easier example. We shall first consider the artists who paint basically what they see. Examples of this kind of art are portraits, seascapes, and landscapes that appear very much like the real thing. The artist here is drawing almost entirely from experiences of what he sees and reproduces it. However, if he decides to introduce other experiences of his self that are inexorably involved with what he is painting and give those visual representation, then the picture will change slightly depending on the amount of these experiences instilled into the original scene. The art, like the author of literature and unlike the newspaper reporter, will include more than what he sees; he will draw upon his total range of experiences, incorporate those into his painting, and present what is commonly referred to as the "artist's interpretation." All the artist is really doing is just painting exactly what he sees, but he is not just seeing the sea or landscape as a camera would see it or as the naked eye would see it, he is taking in the scenery with all the experiences that come to one and not just employing the experience of eyesight only.

Thus, when employing his full faculty of experiences when painting a picture, the artist's view will become different from that which is normally seen. He will be not only painting what he sees but also will be trying to invoke a set of experiences into the picture which will result in not only a visual expression of the artist's experience of what he saw but also a visual representation of the other experiences that interacted with that sight experience of scenery.

HSKL: I believe I'm beginning to understand now and can begin to see the connection with yesterday's discourse. What you have just described to me are the cases of a painter who paints only what he sees and the artist who incorporates other experiences with what he sees and then gives visual representation to the whole. Well, what about art that involves an increasing amount of abstraction?

DTMR: The nature of abstraction in painting, sculpture, or any other form of art has its basis in the artist concerning himself less with those experiences like sight which originate outside the self, and more with those experiences that originate from within the self. It is this attempt to give descriptive expression to the experiences originating from within the self that dictates abstraction. For the most part, a generally non-abstract work representing a beautiful mountain will come out as what we can call "concrete" because we can also stand and view that mountain with our own eyes and see almost the same thing as the artist. Hence, when he paints his picture of it, it bears a good resemblance to what we also see. Thus, we readily understand the picture as it parallels closely our experience, and consequently, we can understand the artist's own experience and be able to use the word "concrete" when discussing that particular piece of canvas. However, should the artist begin to care less what he sees in front of him and begin to concern himself with, for instance, the emotions, feelings, contemplations, or even meditations that the beauty of the mountain causes to issue forth within him, his concern to give these visual representations will cause the picture of the mountain to drastically undergo a metamorphosis that is manifested through abstractions.

HSKL: This is very interesting, but I still cannot fully grasp the nature of the abstraction.

DTMR: Take for example the terms "liberty," "justice," "truth," and the like. Are they abstract words?

HSKL: Yes, of course.

DTMR: And are words like "mountain," "river," "house," and "tree" terms of a concrete nature?

HSKL: Yes, certainly.

DTMR: Well, the difference between these two types of words is that one set is realized through experiences that originate exterior to the self, and those terms that are considered abstract are words that are formed to represent experiences that come from within the self. Now, of course, let me make a slight qualification of this, that being that all words cannot be divided strictly into those two categories as almost all experiences interact with each other and the experiences from without interact with those from within the self. Even the example of a book can be traced to experiences both abstract and concrete. The sight, feel, etc., of a book are, obviously, a concrete experience, but the input of those concrete perceptions causes in the mind the idea of a book to evolve; hence, this experience of the book originating from within is abstract.

HSKL: Anyway, you were speaking of the kinds of words and the nature of abstraction.

DTMR: Yes. It is a word like "justice" or "truth" that has no concrete model which is available to view and observe but is an experience totally abstract and originating from within. When an artist endeavors to give representation to one of these experiences, it naturally will present itself in an abstract way as his experience is very personal and has no particular analogous form existing in the world that we may view.

Hence, when observing the artist's final abstract product, in order to understand it we must evoke our own inner experiences, examine them, and see if our own experiences might identify with the artist's work. If it is truly a powerful work of art, the work itself will cause us to evoke our own experiences of what is the subject of the artist's representation. Putting dimensions to abstract experiences of the self is a difficult job, and when an artist can skillfully project these impressions onto a canvas or a page, into a piece of sculpture, or whatever, and it is powerful enough to evoke the realization of its expression within ourselves, then surely the value of art becomes apparent.

HSKL: Now, let me see if I have this straight. The abstraction in art is in the description of an experience that originates from within oneself, and because it is a very personal experience with no set concrete model which universally depicts that experience, such as seeing a mountain, the representation may not take on any set form that exists in nature, and hence the use of the term "abstraction" comes into play.

DTMR: I can see that you understand me perfectly.

HSKL: Even though I am beginning to see the nature of the abstraction in art, I am afraid I do not quite understand if it exists in all forms of art. I can easily see that abstraction exists in painting and sculpture, but does it extend itself to literature?

DTMR: In literature abstraction is not apparent, but still, it is there. In painting, abstraction takes a visual form that strikes the eye with its irregularities. However, literature deals in words that are formless in themselves. Hence, it is not so strikingly apparent. But, Haskell, one often reads material that deals in what the reader will term "abstract" and "obscure." When an author deals with those experiences of internal origin, he becomes just as "abstract" and "obscure" as the painter. For instance, the obscurity of poetry is quite prevalent and noticeable, would you not say?

HSKL: Yes, I believe I would.

DTMR: The cause of this "obscurity" is nothing else than the author's attempt to depict something very personal and something that is experienced deep within the author and is better denoted as abstraction.

HSKL: I see. Hence, knowing the nature of abstraction in art provides the sight into what leads the painter to deviate from what he sees by eyesight and produce something that is different from the model he is using. The reason for this is that the painter incorporates onto the canvas those experiences that have come to his consideration while viewing the subject of painting. Besides the object of his drawing, there may come into play other experiences that interact with the sight of the subject, and the artist may want to express these feelings, emotions, thoughts, meditations, etc., that he experiences in relation to the subject of his painting.

DTMR: Precisely. However, do not forget that what you have said applies not only to painting but to all forms of art.

HSKL: How is that, Detmar?

DTMR: The nature of abstraction is the basis or reason why all forms of art do not exactly express what is seen in the world. In the same way that the painter adds the experiences that are relative to what he is depicting, the author of a work of literature will add his total set of related experiences to the subject to which he is relating. That is, there is a subject of a work of art: in the painter's case, let us suppose it is a mountain, and for the author's let us suppose it is the same mountain. The painter will see the mountain and will not only want to depict the mountain as he views it but will also want to add those other experiences which are derived from the mountain. These experiences can be of almost any kind, but they will all have to be somehow related to the mountain as it is the subject of the painting.

Some examples of related experiences that the artist may feel would be the awe that the mountain instills within him when he observes it – hence, a terribleness when seeing the mountain. In these areas, he again must try to convey onto the canvas his own personal experiences that are involved with the subject of his painting, the mountain, and these experiences of terribleness or of subtle beauty must be included somehow on the canvas. It is the addition of these related experiences that gives the abstraction to the subject of the picture, and consequently, the subject of the picture will change according to the degree of abstraction added. In literature, the author will relate not only how he sees the mountain by his eyesight but also, like the painter, may want to incorporate his related experience of awe, the subtle beauty of the mountain, or the feeling that the mountain has a terribleness about it. These additions of the author's own related experiences as they become more personal and abstract may well be different from another person's related experiences of the mountain. Thus, what will be expressed by the author may not bear much resemblance to another person's experiences of viewing the same mountain.

HSKL: You keep mentioning the "subject" of the painting or the "subject of the piece of literature" and so on. What do you mean by "subject"? Or do you mean what is often called the "theme" of a work of art?

DTMR: Yes, I suppose so. Although I do not use that word "theme," every work of art has a subject, a center, or a core from which it radiates and expands, and all the experiences depicted and expressed within are related. It's the core that provides the glue that relates the expression of one experience to another and provides the basis for coherency and consistency within the work of art. Just as I mentioned in the example of the painter and his mountain, the subject is the mountain, and all that is depicted on the canvas must have some involvement with the artist's experience of the mountain. Obviously, if the subject is the mountain, to add representations of something that has nothing to do with the mountain would be incongruent.

HSKL: Yes, I absolutely agree, but I am wondering why you do not use the word "theme"?

DTMR: I have no objection to the word in that the meaning is appropriate for our use here when we talk about the "subject" of the work of art. In fact, it may even be a more suitable word. But, recently, I think there is perhaps a tendency among some scholars to possibly over-intellectualize when in discussion of the theme of a certain piece of art. We have established already that each work of art has a subject, or a theme if you will, and for our purposes here today let us stop there and not enter into an inquiry that would examine to what extent and how a theme should be treated. Let us leave the employment of criticism and intellectualizing of works of art to the appropriate scholar, and concern ourselves specifically with the nature and essence of art.

HSKL: I agree. Let's return to the subject of examining our theory of art. I think that would be more interesting and satisfying. Hence, from here I would like to ask about the various schools of painting that have appeared throughout history, such as impressionism, realism, surrealism, and others. What is the nature of these different types of art and can we understand them in terms of our definition of art?

DTMR: Yes, I believe so. First, by recalling our definition of art – which is the expression of how one sees the world, or strictly speaking, the representation of one's total set of experiences concerning any particular subject, and secondly, by recalling that the abstractions of art are due to the expression of those experiences that are most personal and originate within the self. If these two postulations are fully understood, we can realize that these are groups of painters whose way of seeing the world is similar, and consequently there evolves the use of a common method which can be seen throughout their individual works.

HSKL: How is that?

DTMR: Suppose, for instance, that a painter who is known as an impressionist is depicting a seascape. That artist does not just paint what he sees by his eyesight alone; he tries to invoke onto his canvas other feelings (abstractions) that may come to him during the interval of representing the scene. These feelings that he experiences while painting may be of the nature of impressions that the scene leaves upon his mind, and in order to express this scene plus those related feelings (abstractions) that he experiences while observing the subject matter, he will employ a certain technique that he has invented that will help facilitate the expression he desires to communicate, or he will take advantage of a method that is already in use and has already evolved through previous painters who also want to express similar experiences.

HSKL: Excuse me, but could you explain what you mean when you speak of an evolution of method? I would still like to hear what is the nature of a school of painting and why would it come to be that a series of painters would paint in the same style. I am quite in the dark about understanding these points.

DTMR: Well, the reason one painter may adapt or create his own style is that it helps him readily to represent what he wants to express. If the painter is a brilliant one, he will be able to create it by himself and it will naturally evolve from the artist's own particular needs in expression. After him, other artists may recognize his brilliance, and they may also see things similar to the original artist and then employ his style to see if it will help facilitate the things that they would like to depict on their canvases.

In the case of impressionism, the method of expression may be stated to be the dabs and strokes of whole, real, and strong colors intended to give a vividness of the strength of light in order to evoke a subjective and subtle impression. This method will naturally come to be employed by those artists who want to project onto their works those feelings of the impression of a scene since it will have evolved as the most optimal, efficacious way of relating impressionism. Now, suppose one artist comes to realize a particular method – impressionism – and it is most effectual in relating what he wants to say. Then another artist is impressed by the former and begins to employ the former's style in his own paintings. The reason he might do so is that he may realize in the former's painting the abstractions that were being expressed, and he also may see that the former's method was effectual in his producing the intended result.

Hence, realizing this, the latter artist, who may be concerned with those kinds of feelings, may take it upon himself to employ the former's method as he can see that it would be instrumental in producing his own particular abstractions. The original reason for the spreading of the use of the method is that it is seen and realized to be the most effective method in producing a certain set of abstractions. Of course, we must also realize that this occurrence of particular styles (which can be analyzed as techniques) does not lend itself only to painting but can exist anywhere throughout the whole spectrum of art.

HSKL: Yes, I can begin to understand now the reasons behind the rise of a particular style (or technique) in art. But how could it be that styles can occur anywhere in the entire genre of art?

DTMR: Painting is not alone when we speak of the rise of specific styles; we must also include music, literature, sculpture, or even architecture, pottery, or any area where there is an infusion of art into the process. Where there exists art, there exists the potential for similarities of art. Let us take literature, for example. There have evolved three major styles of expression which are prose, verse, and drama. The author will choose which one best suits him for use in expressing his view of the world. Also, within these three styles of expression, we can find subdivisions of style where more specific similarities of abstractions of different authors may tend to induce a similarity in sentence patterns, diction, and so forth.

HSKL: Well, what will induce the authors to first choose like means of representation such as verse? And secondly, what will be the prevailing factors that will cause even a close similarity in style in the extent that word patterns themselves may come to be similar?

DTMR: Let us go back a bit and remember that the factor that caused the occurrence of similar styles in painting was dealing with abstractions. Of course, those parameters that influence artists to choose something as general as whether the expression should be in the form of prose, verse, or drama will naturally be rather non-specific parameters that find their origin in general, vague experiences of a common kind. However, moving to examine similar styles within the confines of, say, verse, we find that the parameters begin to become more specific as we must get closer to the understanding of the author's abstractions. That is, the essence of the parameters that produce similarities, however specific or general within works of art, lies in the similarity of experiences that operate on the self of the artist. The experiences that produce the desire to write in verse will of course be very general, and the interplay of experiences with the workings of the mind will produce the factors that construct the development of the way the artist sees the world. Hence, he will choose a way or style that will be most conducive to permitting what he wants to express – all the way from the general style, such as verse, down to the selection of phrases and individual words.

The workings of external experiences upon the mind and the experiences that originate in the mind will affect the artist's complete style. The reason for the occurrences of similarities in style are that, although the constitutional makeup of one artist may be very different from another since they have in common that they are both human beings, much of their internal makeup will be similar, many of their experiences will be common, and much of any one common experience will be alike. Hence, the abstractions that they may wish to express may be similar, and thus, a style that facilitates a relation of similar abstractions will tend to come into use and evolve as a useful tool in the creation of a work of art.

HSKL: Very interesting, Detmar. I can realize the assertion that there can exist a similarity in style within any kind of art, but can this exist perhaps even in such things as the art of architecture, pottery, or any area where we seem to notice an infusion of the essence of art into a process? Would you explain for me how a likeness of style can evolve into something like architecture, pottery, or even weaving? Also, I wonder how it is that they contain elements of art if they are forms of art at all. That is, what do you suppose is meant by "the art of such and such" – e.g., the art of poetry, the art of interior design, the art of the Japanese tea ceremony, the art of weaving, the art of this craft or that, or anything else which appears not to be pure art, but nevertheless has that feeling about it which brings one to think of it as a kind of art?

DTMR: Yes. Well, in order to answer those questions, I think we should first recall our postulation that art is the expression of how one sees the world, and then look for signs of this in the processes in question. Secondly, we must realize that painting, literature, sculpture, etc., have only the purpose of conveying the expression of the artist's experiences, and that architecture, pottery, weaving, etc., have another purpose for their necessity of being. Behind each of these skills or crafts, the primary purpose is different from that of art, which is just to relate the artist's view of the world. A simple example of this is pottery. The primary purpose of making, for instance, a vase is to hold something; the vase is basically a functional item. However, as a maker of the vase becomes skillful, and as demand increases, and if he has enough time, he will be able to add how he sees the world to the limited capacity that pottery allows for expression. The room for expression lies in both the shape of the vase and in the way the exterior can be designed. Naturally, the form of the vase will have a direct relation to function, but let us not forget that that can be one way of how the artist will perceive the world, the world here being limited to the form of a vase. That is, the potter will see the form of the vase in terms of that which is most functionally suitable for a certain purpose whether it be to hold water, to hold flowers, or whatever; the vase will be made with the idea of seeing form in terms of utility, which is one point of view that would be expressed just as the painter expresses his view, whatever it may be, upon a canvas.

Thus, we may say that no matter how basic or simple a piece of pottery may be when the artisan begins to give form to clay, the rudimentary beginnings of art can begin to appear. All it takes to effect the induction of the process of producing something artistic is the rudiments of expressing one's experiences (internal and external) even if those experiences are restricted to a certain quantity, few in number, but unrestrained in terms of quality. Consequently, when the first artisan long ago, out of dire need for a vessel that would hold water, food, or the like, applied his experiences and creative processes (which, do not forget, are experiences in themselves) to some clay and gave birth to a crude utensil that performed the job he had in mind, the object that he created had the rudimentary beginning of art because the lines that he formed were manifestations of his experiences, although extremely limited. Thus, at this stage, the beginnings of art are barely perceivable but nevertheless exist, since that first artisan employed his own creative processes and was able to manifest these abstractions by making his simple vessel. From this point, the artist may improve upon himself and begin to realize more about pottery and what would be more useful and functional. He would, consequently, proceed to create more mature items through his growing experience, and as the artisan advances, the manifestations of art will become more numerous and powerful in their expressiveness.

HSKL: Interesting. Could you give me another example? Say, architecture?

DTMR: When the architect begins to apply his experiences of space, efficiency, strength, material shape, and all the other things that he deals with to the construction of a building, he is clearly giving vent to a certain area or section of experience. Hence, we may realize the art of architecture. Of course, when compared to a painter or a sculptor, he may be restricted by those parameters of experience of efficiency, space, materials, etc. that he must deal with when designing a building or whatever. Thus, his art is limited in a fashion, but nevertheless, he is in a controlled manner giving expression to his experiences and delineating how he sees a certain part of the world. Therefore, we may say that there exists, here in architecture, art. The problem is the same as what we were discussing yesterday concerning what is literature and what is not. The same reasoning can be applied here because all literature is a form of art.

HSKL: Please, could you recall that part of the discussion for me?

DTMR: We were discussing whether different kinds of writing we were to consider are literature, and the conclusion was that, if the author employs those experiences that originate within himself (abstractions) along with those of the exterior – that is, involves his entirety representing his view of a subject of his world through writing – he is producing literature, a form of art. Also, we have seen that a newspaper article, a telex, etc., are not within the realm of art for the reason that they do not include the total gamut of the author's experiences, and thus, do not contain any abstractions that characterize not only literature but all of art.

In pottery, when the artisan begins to infuse his total set of experiences (and hence, abstractions) into creating pottery, he is essentially instilling the essence of art in his work. Consequently, it is the incorporation of abstractions into pottery (or architecture, weaving, etc.) that adds the quality and essence of art.

HSKL: At what stage do pottery and architecture take on this essence of art? In other words, when do they take on the abstractions of the artisan or the architect?

DTMR: The artisan steps into the realm of art when he goes beyond the basic and standard container that the knows to be a vase, proceeds past that, adds how he perceives an appropriate vase and lends to one a design that comes from within and fulfills the purpose of the vase. That is, before him, there have been other vases and an idea of a vase has already been understood and derived from the specific wants and needs of those who use vases. The artisan comes along, and either he perceives a new design through his experience that is able to demonstrate or fulfill the artisan's perception of a vase which must fulfill certain qualifications demanded by the users, or the demands change and the use of the vase becomes diversified and the artisan must create a new design that will meet the new needs. At this point, the artisan is incorporating his own abstractions by means of new forms into his work – and hence, the presence of art. The artisan will have expressed (through his total set of experiences) how he sees a specific subject in his world. But the key to whether a certain artisan becomes an artist is in his creativity or in his ability to bring forth abstractions. If he just reproduces what has gone before him he is but a copier. However, if he has the ability to see new ways of abstraction, he lends the notion of art to his work. Naturally, the same would hold true for the architect and the like.

HSKL: I see. You mentioned a little while ago that "since that first artisan employed his own creative processes and was able to manifest these abstractions" he qualified himself to be placed in our category of the artist. You have seemed to maintain a direct and positive link between the abstraction and the creating of art.

But also, you have referred to this creative process you mentioned and its relation to the process of art. I wondered if you could explain to me what exactly is the relation between creativity and art and whether creativity is always art.

DTMR: Well, I think creativity can be simply expressed as a process from within the artist's expression of his experiences or abstractions. As you know, "creativity" is often referred to when speaking of artists. We have often heard people speak of "the creativity" of this artist or "the creativity" of that artist, and when we examine art, we can clearly see that within, there is, obviously, the creativity of the artist and that it derives itself from the artist's expression of not only his abstractions but the whole gamut of experiences that he is relating.

HSKL: Yes, I can clearly see that.

DTMR: Of course, everybody has various kinds of experiences: those that originate from outside the self and then are perceived by the self, those experiences that arise from within that are stimulated by other experiences usually from without (for example, love, sadness, grief, happiness, etc.), and those that can spontaneously come from within (for example, divine inspiration, meditation, pure thought, etc.). When the artist begins his expression, he draws upon his experiences, but he must first go through the process of recognizing and associating the relationship of the various experiences before he goes through the trials of expression; that is, it involves the composition of different experiences, and it is there that the creativity exists.

Let me give you an example. Let us say that an artist has the experience that all men are mortal and he knows that Socrates is a man. It is creativity that enables one to see these two experiences in light of an association and be able to connect them and conceive the idea to use them together. Once they are together, it takes the intelligence of the mind to see and realize the conclusion that Socrates is a mortal, but it is the genius of creativity that puts them together in the first place. Now of course it does not have to be a creative genius that can associate those two knowns together, but that is the essence of creativity, and as the less obvious associations of experiences become joined together for consideration, the more the genius of creativity becomes apparent.

HSKL: Do you suppose there is creativity without art?

DTMR: Since there must be expression in order to find art, I suppose there can be creativity without art. A person can go through the process of creating something without expressing it. However, if he chooses to give expression to his creativity and communicate it in some way, then it will become one form of art or another.

HSKL: I see. But I wonder, just for the sake of making it a little clearer in my mind, if you could give me another example of the process of creativity?

DTMR: Surely. Let us take the example of the author who knows the signs, feelings, etc., of avarice who also has experienced and known a person (or persons) who is seemingly a nice, good person but nevertheless embodies the spirit of greed and avariciousness. The creative genius of the author will be able to combine his total set of experiences that concern themselves with such a spirit and enable him to be able to compose a character in his mind that embodies his set of experiences; then he is able to set forth on the task of expression.

HSKL: I see. By the way, were you thinking of any particular artist and character?

DTMR: Yes, I was. I was thinking of the character of Pecksniff in Dickens' Martin Chuzzlewit. As you must realize, the character of Pecksniff in the artist's mind is a composite of experiences of the author, and the creative genius of Dickens was able to gather these experiences together and form the character of Pecksniff. However, even if Dickens were drawing this character from one source only or from one person that he knew in his life, within the knowing of that one person he would still have to compose and assimilate a whole series of experiences, as even the knowing of one person is in itself a complicated series of experiences. Let us take, for example, the character of David Copperfield, which is generally thought to parallel approximately the life of Dickens himself when he was young. Even if the author directly creates a character that closely resembles himself, within that character (or actually within himself) there is still a whole set of experiences that must be connected, associated, and integrated so that a congruous character can be formed. Creativity still plays an important role here, even if what is being formed comes almost directly from oneself. As long as the artist is expressing how he sees the world, then he is employing artistic creativity.

HSKL: Thank you. I think I can fully understand this business of creativity. What I would like to inquire into now is the meaning of this word "expression," since we have been using this word so often, yet at least on my part, without a complete understanding of it.

DTMR: Yes. I am glad you brought this up. Expression is an interesting subject that we should take the time to pursue as it is closely allied with creativity.

HSKL: What do you mean when you say the word "expression," and what is the nature of it?

DTMR: All expression is composed of two dimensions: one is what I call the element of delineation and the other is composition.

HSKL: How is that?

DTMR: Well, it is my opinion that expression is composed of these two factors. In written expression, the element of delineation is the single word or diction. The choice of a word begins the expression and by itself communicates very little, but nevertheless has a certain force behind it. After the selection of one word, another is placed beside it, and then we have the beginning of composition. Hence, the combination of elements of delineation gives composition and the ability to communicate and express completely.

HSKL: What about other forms of expression – like painting or music?

DTMR: Painting is no different. An artist in the process of expression first draws a line of delineation which may in itself hold some expressiveness. The artist draws a second line which is again of the first dimension of communication as was the first, but the placement of it in relation to the first line adds the second dimension of expression, which is composition. Both dimensions are necessary for complete communication, but the thought processes behind each are different, as within paintings there can be seen different emphasis placed upon calligraphy (the first dimension), or in another painting, there can be seen perhaps a strong emphasis on composition where the line becomes less important.

HSKL: Yes, that is true now that I think of it. I have examined many paintings in the history of art classes, and I can now remark that the emphasis on calligraphy and composition certainly changes from artist to artist, although I never thought of it in those terms. In some paintings, the line is quite sharp, strong, and well-delineated, and composition may not be so strong. However, in another artist's paintings, we can find almost no distinction of line and heavy reliance on composition. And if I might say so following what we have discussed so far, the reasons that compel the artist to use one of the dimensions of expression more heavily than the others would be that he sees the world in a particular way, and the use of one dimension more than another is just the manifestation of his experience and internal makeup and helps facilitate his expression in the manner he would like to communicate.

DTMR: I can see you understand it completely.

HSKL: However, you mentioned that all forms of expression are made up of these two dimensions. What about music?

DTMR: Yes, of course. The note would correspond to the word or the line, and the addition of a second note would add the dimension of composition. I should say that within the first dimension of expression, there are factors that can add to or detract from the force of the note, the line, or the word. For example, a line can be drawn boldly, weakly, or with strong color or light color, etc. The word can be changed to a stronger word with the same meaning (e.g., make, force, compel); it can be underlined or capitalized; or if it is read out loud, a voice emphasis can influence its effectiveness immensely. The single note of music enjoys a wide range of variance in its one-dimensional effectiveness. It can be played by a violin, a guitar, or a flute, and it can be played by any one instrument with a harshness, with a kind of gusto, or it can be played with a softness or in a myriad of other interpretations.

HSKL: Yes, I can see that these two dimensions of expression remain consistent in whatever medium is used. But I would like to inquire into the art of music a little further since it has come up in the conversation and since we have not spoken much about it in spite of the fact that it is one of the major forms of art.

DTMR: Yes, please proceed.

HSKL: I wondered if I might ask if the essence of the art of music is of the same nature as that of painting, literature, and indeed all of art, or is it separate and something whose nature we cannot know.

DTMR: Well, Haskell, I think there is no doubt that music is a form of art and that the essence of art runs consistently throughout all of art, or else it certainly would not be the essence.

HSKL: Yes, I agree.

DTMR: Consequently, music, being an art, is not separate in essence and is of the same ilk and nature.

HSKL: Yes, of course.

DTMR: Music also, like any other art, is the expression of the composer's experiences upon a certain subject (or theme if you will), but the medium which he uses to communicate his experiences is through sound.

HSKL: Detmar, surely you will not be so brash and, really, overly self-assertive here by claiming that music is a direct expression from the experience of the composer. I am aware that there are those that believe that music has some relationship to deep feelings and thoughts, but their grounds for believing so are rather tenuous, and even they would concede that the relationship is not perfect and not so direct as you seem to hold that it is. And on the other side of the coin, there are those who adamantly believe that music has no connection with feeling and thought and is of an entirely different source, although they cannot determine what. Hence, one group of music theorists believes music is related to some sort of inner emotions and feelings and tries to express these, and another group believes music does not present, relate, or express any such feeling, emotion, or whatever and is wholly without embodiment, is perfectly intrinsic, and – as some would say – perfectly abstract. Also, I must say that I myself tend to lean that way since I know that when I sit and listen to even a most famous piece of music, I am not aware of any evocation of any specific feeling or emotion that comes from the music. Nor, do I realize any certain thought, pleasure, or experience (if I may) that is evoked by the music. Hence, I must for myself make the conclusion that music does not have any specific tie with experience, and if I am to be consistent with the postulates that we have agreed upon so far concerning the nature of art, I must say then that music must not be a form of art, but I know and feel absolutely that that conclusion is absurd and that certainly music must be and is a form of art. Thus, I am unsure now of our postulates and am now of the opinion that somewhere we have gone wrong.

DTMR: Well, I can understand your doubt. Now let's see if we can find some solution to the problem, as we both agree that music is definitely within the realm of art.

HSKL: It would interest me to no end.

DTMR: The first thing I must put forth, as we have already postulated, is that experience provides all the raw material for expression in art. Thus, I will make the further postulation that the artist is nothing but a certain set of experiences – that is, the artist's being is the summation of his experiences.

HSKL: How would that be, Detmar?

DTMR: Well, as we have found yesterday, we can distinguish all experiences into groups. The first are those that we receive from outside the self: these experiences originate from without, then are perceived and sensed by the self, and hence are incoming experiences. Examples of this kind are numerous and easy to recognize. If you touch something, or see a mountain, or hear somebody speak, then you are realizing an experience of the first kind. I do not think I need to go into this further. You can readily grasp this, of course.

HSKL: Yes, I follow you perfectly. It is what makes up the second group that I may not be able to understand completely.

DTMR: The second group is made up of those experiences that originate from within the self, and examples of these are anger, love, sadness, happiness, joy, thought, etc. However, within these experiences of the self, there are two types. One type are those that are responses to outside experiences, and the other are realizations that require no outside stimulus and originate spontaneously from within. An example of the first group is anger. Suppose somebody hits you and you become angry. The experience of being hit is, obviously, a realization that has come to you from without, and in response to it a reaction spontaneously springs up inside of you and that is anger. The sight of food can cause certain spontaneous reactions that a person can experience. Hence, the realization of something exterior initiates or causes an experience to originate in the self, to rise, and be manifested.

Experiences of the second group, of the inner kind, are those that need no direct impetus from the outside and spring from the self spontaneously. Examples of this group are pure thought, meditation, and inspiration – divine or otherwise. These forms of experiences may or may not be stimulated by something outside the self. The thought may easily be induced by something exterior; however, it may at times not be. A person may close off the outside world and concentrate on something within the self – say, a concept, an idea, an inspiration itself – and proceed to consider it using only the thought processes of the mind; in doing so the self is undergoing an experience of the self itself. Essentially, the self is experiencing itself and its own processes of thinking or meditating.

HSKL: Then thinking and meditation are in themselves forms of experience, and the only difference between them and other kinds of experiences is that the origin is different, but they are realized by the self in just the same manner as any other experience.

DTMR: That's correct. Now let us consider inspirations. These movements of intellect produce ideas from within and are the source from which creativity springs. We touched upon this when we spoke of creativity in literature and we examined the example of negative time. The realization of this was a type of inspiration.

HSKL: Excuse me, Detmar, but I am still a bit unclear upon that point, and if you could again go over the concept of creativity, it would help clear up in my mind the present subject of conversation.

DTMR: Yes, certainly. The basis of creativity is the ability to make an extrapolation of two or more experiences to produce something new and original. Let me take something very simple as an example. Suppose you see a mountain (which is one experience) and suppose you also have realized the motion of climbing up. Then it is a quick and easy extrapolation of the self to give forth the idea of climbing to the top of the mountain which you see. Now granted, that does not seem like any momentous piece of creativity, but nevertheless, it is an idea, however simple, that sprang spontaneously from the self and is creative in nature. Obviously, the two experiences that preceded it are of the kind that originated outside the self, but if the self is allowed to consider the realization of these two experiences, then an idea may come forth that is a pure idea, simple though it is, created by the self, inspirational in nature, yet having to be experienced. Its nature is that it sprang from the self and is actually in essence a kind of inspiration.

HSKL: How is it inspirational? There were the two experiences of exterior origin, and these provided the stimulus that gave rise to the idea of climbing the mountain. Hence, I would suppose that the springing forth of this bit of creativity is of the first group, of interior-originating experiences, and not of the second.

DTMR: The reason that we should consider this piece of creativity inspirational is because the self has to actively involve itself and consider the two experiences before anything will appear. If it does not engage itself in the deliberating of the experiences, there would be no hope of the idea coming out. Thus, in the case of the inspirational experiences, exterior experiences will, of course, be present for consideration of the self, but there may or may not be any outcome since there must be some active process enacted by the self to produce any creative result. However, when this result does come, it certainly comes as something that is realized and is experienced by the self. That is, realization is an experience in itself: the self-realizing something is an experience. Of course, how the realization (or the experience) comes to the surface of our awareness or what constitutes the origin and processes that lie beneath the surface of realization – whether it be spiritual, divine, or compound – we cannot know clearly, but we will deem the realization of what comes out an experience of inspirational constituency.

HSKL: Unfortunately, I am still a little unclear about this whole thing. For example, if I am in love with a girl my reactions to her are all, I would think, inspirational in nature, and none would be of the first sort that we mentioned. When I see her, when I consider her in my mind, or when I meet her, I would suppose that my reactions, responses, my thoughts all would be experiences that are inspirational. In other words, are not all creations and responses of love, anger, sympathy, and all other emotions that come from the self-realized in an inspirational manner also? Hence, could not all interior-originating experiences be interpreted as inspirational in nature?

DTMR: Not really, though I understand what you are trying to present. Again, experiences of the first group do not require any consideration of the self. They are simply stimulus-response realizations, and thus, there necessarily must be an exterior-originating experience that directly operates on the self to produce a response that is experienced. Although when the response comes forth and is realized, just as an experience of the second group comes forth and is realized, it is automatic in nature and not inspirational. The inspirational realization requires the active intervention of the self-involving processes and does not require necessarily an exterior-originating realization to produce its creative attainment.

HSKL: Well, a person's involvement in the love of a girl is certainly not just a stimulus-response reaction like that of base animals; surely, you must consider the phenomena of falling in love inspirational and not purely a simple, vulgar reaction. I submit to you that there is consideration of the self here.

DTMR: Haskell, I am sorry I have not made myself clear. Of course, the falling in love is not just a biological chain reaction. But the whole situation is a series of experiences, and if we take the time to break them down into their constituent parts, we will find that of course there are some stimulus-response experiences and some other realizations of the inspirational sort. I am only trying to show the various types of experiences.

HSKL: I see, and am now satisfied for the most part on this matter of inspirational experiences. But what about the process of logic? Is it inspirational in nature?

DTMR: We are carrying this subject too far. Logic by itself is not inspirational. It is a phenomenon of nature and can be found in the self, in a computer, or in an adding machine. The important thing to understand here is the essence of creativity. Inspiration just refers to the spontaneous realizations of experience that come from within. They can be of various natures, such as a religious inspiration where a person may spontaneously realize an experience of faith in God; inspiration can be possibly an idea created by an author realizing a new character, or by a mathematician realizing a new concept from his calculations. In any case, it just refers to the realization of interior-originating experiences.

HSKL: Well, I believe I have finally grasped the distinction of the different kinds of experiences. However, you spoke just a bit ago about creativity, but you discussed it in general and not in the context of art. Is the creativity of art any different?

DTMR: No, of course not. Creativity in art is just as we mentioned yesterday. The artist takes those exterior-originating experiences which he is painting, or about which he is writing, or which he is in some other way giving expression and adds to it those interior-originating realizations which he understands to be irrevocably entwined with those exterior-experiences. The added expression of those interior realizations refers to the abstractions of the artist that we talked about yesterday. The means by which the artist realizes the related interior-originating experiences and correlates them to the exterior-experiences are inspirational and creative in nature (and also an experience in itself).

HSKL: Ah! I am beginning to understand the meaning of all this. But at this point, just for clarification, could you give me an example?

DTMR: Surely. Suppose we have an artist of sorts who tends to see things in numbers; that is, he is always seeing the world in abstractions of numerical denominations. One day this fellow is standing at the edge of a field that has a cow in it. This fellow looks upon this cow in terms of the number 1, and thus, "1" is standing in a field. Then, another "1" wanders in from an adjacent field and our friend immediately applies what he already knows how to do – addition. In his mind as soon as the second "1" enters the field he takes each "1" and adds them together, and he symbolizes it when he chooses to express it as $1 + 1 = 2$. If again a third cow walks into the field, the process again repeats itself. So far, all this of course directly relates itself to experience, and to what our mathematical artist sees. Now, let us suppose that our artist has never seen the situation where some cows stand in a field and one or more leave. Suppose he has never experienced this, but today he does. There are three cows standing in the field and all of a sudden for no apparent reason, one of them leaves.

HSKL: You're being facetious.

DTMR: Sorry. If I seem so, please excuse me, but there is a point here about which I am wholly serious. When that cow leaves, it suddenly comes to him that there are only "2" left, and he has realized another mathematical process and hence will describe it in his expression as 3 1 = 2; thus, he will have advanced to two mathematical processes. Our artist who sees his world in terms of mathematics has realized subtraction through interpreting what he has experienced by employing his intelligence, which is fine in itself and is the first step to creativity. However, to reach a pure form of creativity, suppose our thinker does not wait for the cow to leave but extrapolates in his mind the situation that if one cow can enter the pasture, which he has heretofore described as "plus (+)," one or more cows can leave as well. He then sets up the hypothetical situation with a minus sign and realizes the process of subtraction before he actually encounters the exterior-originating experience; hence, he predicts its existence. The second situation is inspirational and wholly creative in nature and is one kind of experience in itself.

HSKL: Then the process of subtraction is or is not created from experience?

DTMR: Our artist friend realizes subtraction through extrapolating other similar experiences and applying them to the present situation. He may, for instance, have himself walked in and out of a room, pasture, or whatever, and hence, from the experience of walking and from the awareness of being able to go in and out of something, he can realize a predictable situation and create an expression of it – in this case, 3 1 = 2.

HSKL: Then creativity is just this extrapolation of experience.

DTMR: Yes.

HSKL: Then how does this relate to art? Where in art does creativity present itself in the same way as the creating of mathematical processes which our adept friend was so quickly able to excogitate?

DTMR: Creativity in art is no different. Just as our excogitator (who is actually an artist if he puts expression to his creativeness) was able to extrapolate already known experiences of walking and going out of something to a cow leaving the other cows, the realizing of the probable action of one of the cows leaving making the remainder number "2" (an interior-originating experience), thereby realizing the process of subtraction (which, mind you, is only a symbolic representation of the experience), the artist, in the same way, extrapolates his inner originating experiences to other realizations and then expresses these as abstractions in his representations of presumable situations which are relations of how he sees the world.

HSKL: Could you explain that again? I am not sure I completely understand.

DTMR: Sure. As we know, creativity in art is often said to be inspirational in nature, and so it may well be, but the important thing that should be grasped when trying to form a concrete understanding of the nature of creativity is that it is a form of experience that originates within the self and its internal formation and realization is an experience in itself. Also, the constitutional makeup of creativity is the application of intellectual movement to previous or present experiences which results, when expressed in art, in how the artists see the world through presumable, created situations based upon experiences. Hence, in art, the creativity lies in integrating to a subject of exterior-originating realizations the artist's applicable interior-originating experiences which manifest themselves as abstractions and present a probable creative situation representing how the author or painter sees the world through his experiences.

HSKL: Yes, I'm beginning to understand you now, but I can't quite figure out what you mean by the word "presumable" that you have mentioned when speaking of creativity.

DTMR: Of course, you have noticed that in literature or in other forms of art what the author describes, relates, draws, or whatever does not necessarily correlate precisely to what ostensibly has happened in his life. For example, a painter does not always paint exactly what he sees and an author does not always write strictly autobiographically. We have already seen that this is due to the incorporation into the author's expression of the use of abstraction and this is the source and essence of his creativity; when this occurs the situation or the subject that he is expressing becomes presumable.

HSKL: In what sense?

DTMR: In the sense that all that is expressed is taken from experience. Just as our thinker watching the cows devises subtraction to express one cow leaving – which he has not yet actually seen but knows through correlative experiences to be a presumable situation that he may express through his arithmetic – we may say that all the constituent parts of what the artist describes are directly taken from experience, and the conglomerate of this myriad of realization is a creative situation which strictly speaking may not have occurred per se but is nevertheless known through experience.

HSKL: Yes, I believe I am beginning to grasp the point. Just as our mathematician-artist is able to devise and then express subtraction to express what might happen in a cow pasture, the novelist, poet, etc., will describe selected presumable situations of his own, excogitated through his creativity. But what about a painting or a sculpture or any work of art that is visual in expression as opposed to written? How can visual works be considered presumable? If a painter draws a picture of Mount Fuji in Japan and then inculcates his creative abstractions to produce only semblances of the Mount Fuji that we actually see, then how can we understand this to be presumable as there is no potential of this occurring? Whereas there is a potentiality of one of the cows leaving the field and hence realizing our friend's calculations, or there is a potentiality that what an author of a novel describes could actually also occur and that a character, as he describes, in reality, could appear and hence corroborate the potentiality of the work?

DTMR: One must keep in mind that what is expressed by the artist is how he sees the world; therefore, the potentiality in a painting exists in the expression of experiences that present how the artist realizes his world. You understand the artist's expression to have a potentiality in actual occurrences, like the possibility of our mathematician's expression coming true by seeing the leaving of the field of one of the cows, thereby fulfilling the potentiality of what was expressed. However, the potentiality in art lies not so much in the possibility of its actually occurring, but in its representing a reality or an understanding through experience of how one sees the world. Thus, when an author writes a work of literature or a painter paints a picture, the potentiality of the work of art lies in the work being realized and understood in purporting a certain reality particular to that artist. It is when the artist combines his experiences and creativity to produce a work of art that presents a certain way of seeing the world, and when this certain view of one's world and the experiences and abstractions included is then realized and seen by the observer of art as an expression of a particular piece of reality (this can be anybody who appreciates and examines the work, including the artist himself when it comes to him that he has realized and understood his own work), it can be said that the potentiality of the piece of art is realized.

HSKL: Well, thank you. I have now gained, I believe, an understanding of this idea of potentiality in art. But now let's return, if we might, to what brought this discussion about – that is, the question of the basis of creativity – and find out whether all art, including music, is based on experience.

DTMR: Yes, I remember quite clearly, and now is the time to return to the original problem and see if we can make any sense of it all.

HSKL: I am particularly bothered by the idea that the basis of music lies in experience.

DTMR: Well, we have just now seen that the raw material of creativity is experience, to which is applied the artist's power of extrapolation to produce his own particular expression of his world, and in this one can see the creativity in art. But the important point at the moment is understanding that the raw material of creativity lies nowhere but in experience, and no matter if we are speaking of the creativity of painting, literature, sculpture, or even music, mathematics, or philosophy, the basic element on which the inspirational creativity of the self works is experience. (And by the way, creativity itself is, as we have seen, a realization and all realizations are experiences.) Hence, it must be seen that even in music the creation of a theme by a composer has its roots in experience.

HSKL: Well, that certainly follows from our understanding of the basis of creativity. Thus, I probably should concede that music is steeped in experience, but what kind of experience would music come from? It certainly cannot be experienced like those used by other artists, like those of a painter of landscapes, and like those of an author of a novel, as they are usually concrete experiences that I can understand and readily grasp. The experiences that provide the basic material from which the composer draws and expresses himself are certainly not the experiences we have been discussing.

DTMR: Yes, Haskell, you are right to some extent, I would say. Obviously, the composer does not work on the same level of consciousness and works not so much with the exterior-originating experiences but wholly with abstractions that, when expressed, bear little or no resemblance to anything that is readily recognizable since there is no direct employment of the exterior-originating experience. But that is not to say that the exterior-originating experience plays no part in the composer's art. That which originates from without the self works upon and influences the inner realizations of the artist (or anybody for that matter), and naturally, the exterior interacts with the self and exerts influences. However, because the composer deals strictly with abstraction, the final product expressed in musical notes will of course be abstract in nature and not bear any readily recognizable resemblance to experience.

HSKL: Then it would seem that the greater the use of the abstraction, the less recognizable it becomes. Also, it would seem that the composer works along the same lines as some contemporary artists of sculpture and painting who also deal extensively with abstractions. Hence, their final expression is not readily seen to have any relation to recognizable exterior experiences.

DTMR: Yes, you are right. But these interior-originating realizations are usually recognizable to some extent, but it is just that they do not have any direct resemblance to exterior-originating experiences.

HSKL: How is that?

DTMR: Well, let us take, for example, some interior-originating experiences such as feelings of love, beauty, or sadness. These, of course, are influenced in some way by exterior-originating realizations.

HSKL: As, for example, with the feeling of love, we would need the exterior experience of a wife, parents, or something else which interacts with the self and thereby provides the stimulus to observe the inner originating experience of love, or with beauty, we would need, say, the sight of nature, or with sadness the loss of a loved one.

DTMR: Right. And because each of us has similar experiences to each other (but, of course, never precisely the same) involving interior-originating experiences such as love, beauty, sadness, etc., and because human beings are similar in their internal makeup, at least in the sense that we can all feel and realize such experiences – though degree and intensity will certainly vary – we may be able to recognize in a very general way such expressions of artists giving vent to these abstractions since we also have had similar interior-originating experiences.

HSKL: What do you mean by "in a very general way," Detmar?

DTMR: The expression of the abstraction, Haskell, is a general process and specifies nothing in particular.

HSKL: I don't follow you.

DTMR: Abstractions as a whole are what we might call general experiences, while exterior realizations are more specific. Although any abstraction is a certain or specific experience in itself, its content is general. I think any example of an abstraction would serve to make my point clear.

HSKL: Yes. Well, let me suggest our previous ones of beauty, sadness, and love.

DTMR: I think anybody would soon be disposed to agree that the feelings of beauty, love, or sadness do not immediately present themselves to clear, lucid definition, and understanding. The sight of a tree or a mountain is much more readily understood and known for what it is, than the feelings of beauty, love, sadness, or liberty, justice, or any other abstraction one might name. Hence, because the abstraction has no embodiment that might easily be recognized, the expression of it will also tend to take an unspecific form. This leads us to the understanding of the reason for subjectivity in expression. When standing before a piece of very highly abstract art, we are likely not to immediately be impressed with objective experiences such as a tree, lake, or mountain. An abstract work of art is likely to invoke within us subjective feelings of sadness, love, or other interior-originating experiences. The abstractions in a work of art will not indicate objective realizations but will bring about subjectivity (if it is an effective, consistent work of art) a recognition of one or more inner originating experiences such as beauty, sadness, love, justice, or any of the myriad of subjective feelings one might hold in conjunction with a particular subject with which a work of art concerns itself. Hence, subjective expression in art relates not a specific delineation of an event or events, but an intangible, impalpable abstraction, and when one views a work of art, in order to sufficiently appreciate the expressions of the abstractions presented, one must approach the piece of art with an open subjectivity that enables one to place his own similar experiences at his disposal to recognize and understand those that the artist is trying to convey.

HSKL: Now, I understand that, but if you would, might you relate this all back to our inquiry on music?

DTMR: Yes, the point that should be remembered is that music is no different from any other highly abstract form of art. Experience is the raw material that enables the artist to make the abstraction and employ this in his art. In music, as we have already seen, expression is through combining tones that are instrumental and/or vocal.

HSKL: Yes, that is quite clear.

DTMR: Next, essential to any piece of music is the theme, heretofore referred to in other kinds of art as the subject. If one is to appreciate a piece of music, he must first recognize the theme, which is an expression of an abstraction, or abstractions, of which the foundation is an inner originating experience or experiences. These experiences may or may not be recognizable as pertaining to any specific subject such as sadness, love, etc., but may be so profound as to have come from the deep recesses of the self where any relation to anything cannot be seen. An artist, and especially the composer, may have the ability to delve so far into his self that the experiences that are realized, when expressed, may not be well understood to have much bearing to any of the usual readily recognizable experiences (such as beauty, liberty, etc.) and may be experiences that run past these into an area of the self where things may not be so well delineated as to be able to attach specific names to describe the abstractions that the artist is able to bring to the surface and express.

Therefore, music (or for that matter any form of art where the abstractions are profound) may or may not have themes that are superficially recognizable or can be associated with universally known interior- (or exterior-) originating experiences, but nevertheless do come from experiences, however deeply realized far down in the self. Hence, when listening to the great music of geniuses such as Beethoven, Mozart, Bach, etc., it is often said – as you yourself, Haskell, pointed out – that one cannot necessarily see any clear connection between the music and experience; it is the profundity to which the composer must reach into his own self in order to draw upon the realizations which will enable him to create such sublime compositions as those of the great composers.

HSKL: Yes, I can understand what you have said so far, and so far you have shown that music does have a connection with experience, although the specific experience may not be recognizable, being of a profound interior realization. However, there is music that does present itself as having associations with various kinds of experiences both interiorly and exteriorly originating. Examples of where associations are made would be lower forms of music such as folk songs. I would like to ask you why it seems that one can soon recognize the presence of experience in folk, country, and western songs, pop songs, and not so with the difficult and higher forms of music. Perhaps if I knew what distinguishes the various kinds of music, I may be able to understand more clearly the reason for this.

DTMR: Haskell, I think you almost answered your own question, and probably if I pressed you for it, you could respond to it fully and adequately yourself as I perceive you have some already established views. But for clarification in your own mind and mine as well, let's discuss the makeup of some of the forms of music and see where that leads us. Let's begin with folk songs.

HSKL: Yes, that would be a good place to start. Many times when listening to specific songs I cannot help but relate to certain experiences which I believe the artists are trying to convey through their music.

DTMR: Yes. Of course, they are trying to relate a certain set of experiences which when expressed convey how the particular artist sees the world. The folk song employs the use of the voice in the singing of words, and both the singing of words and the voice itself communicate experiences in conjunction with the playing of musical notes by an instrument. For example, if the song is of love and the words of the song contain some message concerning some experiences of love, then the listener, of course, cannot help but somehow relate to love.

HSKL: Yes, I can see that.

DTMR: Also, the voice of the singer of the song will try to convey a feeling of love through the tone of his voice and/or through other means of vocal emoting which will contribute to communicating the subject of the song.

HSKL: How would that be?

DTMR: Well, for example, one will not employ a happy, sprightly voice when singing of some lost love, and someone would certainly not make use of a sad, melancholy tone of voice when singing of a newfound love.

HSKL: Yes, certainly.

DTMR: So, I think we may say that a singer can employ his various means of vocal emoting to help produce the desired appropriate effect in the listener.

HSKL: I see. Then, if I may summarize a bit, a song can communicate its experiences through the musical notes, the voice of the singer, and through the words, and the composer's experiences, abstractions, realizations are communicated to express how he sees the world just like any other artist does.

DTMR: Yes, that is correct.

HSKL: It is often said the words to some folk songs are so well expressed that they may stand alone as a piece of art and need not the accompanying music. I wondered, to what extent does the song depend upon the words to communicate the composer's experiences and vice versa.

DTMR: This, of course, will vary greatly from song to song, but we may be sure that they depend on each other and reinforce each other as the composer sees it fit to employ both musical abstractions and vocal/ verbal singing. Of course, whether critics may view the words to any one song as sufficiently powerful enough to stand alone as a work of art is for them to decide, but the artist saw that, in order to be more effective in expressing his own particular views, the use of the combination of music with the voice and words would be more effective.

Now, to proceed to answer your question more precisely, the degree to which the artist will use these factors of voice and music varies greatly, and he may put as much emphasis on one or the other as he wishes. For example, in a particular song, the words may be very important to the conveyance of what the artist wants to express. However, in a different song, the musical development will predominate, and words become less important, while the notes and tones that are conveyed through musical instruments and voice become more important. This situation is noticeable in many kinds of music, and particularly in modern rock and also sometimes in blues songs. The importance of the words diminishes to such an extent in the song that only an understanding of a few significant words that pertain to the general feeling of the song would be sufficient to the purpose of the artist (or artists). In fact, in many rock songs, complete ignorance of the meaning of the words is acceptable as they are not essential to the appreciation and understanding of the artist's work. Only the appreciation of the instrumentation of the musical notes and the vocal notes and tones are sufficient.

HSKL: You mentioned something about the blues.

DTMR: The singing of the blues is a perfect example of this. Even supposing an appreciator of the blues were listening to a song and could not understand the words being sung by the singer, since many times the actual words are not important, that appreciator could understand and recognize the blues of the artist's song by the music and by the vocal intonation. If the artist who is singing the song invokes his ability to sing the blues well, one may quickly recognize the blues that the artist is trying to express without at all understanding the words to the song.

HSKL: But of course, if he did, understanding and appreciation would be all the better, I suppose.

DTMR: Yes of course, if in that particular song, the words were intended to be important and they held significance in that they communicated experiences relevant to the theme of the song.

HSKL: I can now see how the words and their vocalization in a song help to transmit experiences that the composer would intend. But, from here, let's move to the instrumental side of music, as a few questions have arisen in my mind.

DTMR: By all means, let me hear them.

HSKL: First of all, I am wondering what it is that separates and characterizes the various kinds of music. For example, what makes country music and what makes rock music, what makes opera and classical "classical"? Could it possibly be as we have postulated: that the roots of these various kinds of music lie essentially in the experience of the composer?

DTMR: There you go again asking me something to which you already know the answer and can perceive the solution certainly to everybody's satisfaction.

HSKL: It is not that at all, Detmar. Through your insight, I am coming to an understanding of the problem, but it is still not fully developed yet in my mind, so please try to bear with me. Perhaps, at least for the sake of clarification, we could go over the question of the nature of the distinction among the various kinds of music.

DTMR: As you have already perceived, the nature of the differences in the various kinds of music lies in the different kinds of experiences that the composer would like to express in his view of his world, his childhood, his lifestyle, and the entire set of experiences in his life will be the reservoir from which he draws to enable him to compose. However, in music, most of the experiences from which he will draw will be of the inner originating kind, and it is the abstraction of these experiences into notes and tones that constitutes musical expression. Hence, in the case of country music, we find that people of rural backgrounds will be more apt to produce the themes and instrumentation that we know as country music. I think we can say in general that somebody outside an American country-style culture is least likely to compose American country songs, and also least likely to appreciate this style of music; although for somebody outside that country environment, it is certainly not impossible to come to know, like, appreciate it, and even come to compose it through exposure to it. I think it is quite evident that people of different ages, environments, cultures, and experiences will tend to create their own particular musical styles that will express their experiences.

HSKL: Yes, I believe I can see the points you are trying to make. I can understand how folk songs will come from people of a certain culture, and these people will give rise to a certain brand of folk songs that will express a certain set of experiences peculiar to their culture and environment. Also, I can see how this would be true of other forms of music – for instance, the blues. I can understand that the blues would grow out of a certain environment and how blues songs would be expressive of those experiences undergone in that particular environment, and that when one appreciates the blues it is because one can realize and appreciate those experiences that are being expressed within the song. But I have not yet come to understand how this would apply to music such as rock music and classical music. These forms of music seem more universal in terms of those who compose and appreciate them. I'm wondering why that is.

DTMR: You believe that rock and classical, having an almost universal audience, with composers of both types of music coming from various backgrounds, are perhaps different in constitution from folk music, which seems to derive itself from a certain culture – such as Japanese folk music, which is born from a very particular culture and naturally would contain very singular tones, notes and instrumentations peculiar to that country only?

HSKL: Yes. You see my problem.

DTMR: Well, this indeed is a very difficult question. I believe the answer lies in the extent to which the composer abstracts his experiences, and also to the extent that the composer excludes the abstraction of exterior-originating experiences and delves into the self, and extracts and extrapolates his inner originating experiences. The more the composer turns inward and the more he abstracts the more profounder experiences, the more the music will become abstract, and the more the music will have a subtle, sublime universality in its appeal. And it is here we run across the standard by which we may know why the music of Beethoven is intrinsically and inherently better in quality than most folk, country, or pop music. The standard of criteria here is the extent to which the composer has turned inward and abstracted his most profound experiences and developed them into a musical composition. Ultimately, this profundity may possibly go to the actual rhythms, cycles, workings, needs, cravings, and actions of the biological self. That is, if a composer can realize the profound rhythms and workings of the biological self, this is an experience in itself, and when related through notes and tones and instrumentation, the music will have a universal potential for appreciation since human beings are essentially very similar biologically, and this biological similarity may give everybody the potential to be able to appreciate the more profound types of music.

HSKL: But why is it normally true that people of more education and intelligence generally tend to appreciate classical forms of music more than those of less intelligence and education?

DTMR: I believe it is due to the inclination of those people who become more educated to, in general, be more introspective about experiences and to consider their inner selves more often and to a greater degree than those who lack more intelligence and education. If someone of less intelligence and education took the effort and was disposed to be introspective and considered things as far as he could consider, he too would be able to learn and grow to appreciate the higher forms of music – and not only music but all forms of aesthetics.

HSKL: Well, what about rock music? This kind of music is certainly not as profound and with aesthetic value to the extent that classical music is, yet it has an appeal that extends to the youth throughout the world.

DTMR: I think that we may find that the difference between classical music and rock music lies in the instrumentation and development. Many of the themes of rock music are as profound as any to be found anywhere in music.

HSKL: Are you serious?

DTMR: Quite. If you were to take a violin and play on it some of the more famous and profounder themes of rock music, you would find that the theme of the piece of rock music can indeed be as profoundly sublime as the themes of Mozart and Beethoven. However, development in rock music, I must say, is for the most part lacking, and cannot be compared to development in classical music. Also, you will recall what we mentioned a while ago concerning the constitution of a painting: that paintings are made up of two parameters that dictate the entire mode of expression within a piece of art – calligraphy (the line) and composition. This situation exists in all forms of art, and indeed in all expression. First, there is the unit of expression, then the combination of that unit with other units, but of course, each unit itself changes in constitutional essence.

HSKL: I'm not following you.

DTMR: In painting, there is the line and the combination of lines that make up the picture.

HSKL: What about color?

DTMR: Color is a variable inherent within the line and is one of those factors that permit expression by the single unit of the line. The other factors here permitting expression lie in the development of the line – the length, the width, the straightness or the curviness, and the like. Next in the makeup of the picture is composition, which is the position of the various lines in respect to each other.

HSKL: I have one question concerning your "line." What about those painters who do not use the line to convey expression? There are painters who instead of using the stroke of a brush, which would of course convey the line, will not even use a brush and may just splatter, pour, or transfer the paint onto the canvas by any one of several means none of which would be the stroke of the brush; hence, we may find round blotches in the picture. This certainly is not a line; thus, I would be tempted to think that, in addition to the line, there is a myriad of other ways by which a painter may express form and thereby make composition.

DTMR: Well, perhaps there is some confusion in the use of the word "line" if one thinks of the line in the conventional sense. I suppose I should have said "the transferences of form onto the canvas" instead, and a combination of the expressed forms would result in composition. If we want to broaden our first unit of expression to include all of visual art, then we certainly would have to broaden the terminology from "line" to "the transferences of form," thereby enabling us to include sculpture or any other visual art.

HSKL: I see. Now, perhaps you could tell me how this business of the parameters of form and composition in the visual arts relates to music or even to the art of literature.

DTMR: Surely. Expression in music is achieved in the same manner as in painting or any other form of art. First, there is the parameter of the unit of expression, which in drawing and in other visual arts are the individual forms and which in music is the note. The constitution of the note varies according to the instrument that plays it (hence the change in tone), the intensity, and the length of time it is played. For example, a note played on a violin will naturally have different characteristics than a note played on an electric guitar. Next in music expression is, obviously, the combination of the notes, and thus, comes composition. In literature, expression is actualized by the unit, the word. The word, like the musical note or the line, etc., may change in its intensity of meaning and of expressiveness and is usually referred to as diction. Of course, the combination of words begins the process of composition.

HSKL: Very interesting, Detmar. Though I wonder if perhaps we could turn to why this discussion of the two essential parameters of expression, the mode of unit and composition, is significant.

DTMR: The understanding of these two parameters helps to clarify the makeup of expression in art and helps to shed light on what constitutes different styles within art. First, let us take the painting of the picture. Some artists rely heavily on the line as it may facilitate what they want to express. Heavy reliance on the line would tend to indicate a bold, brazen, forceful, objective, clear-cut feeling in expression of the piece of art. A heavy reliance on composition and de-emphasis of the line would tend to be indicative of a subtler, gentler, softer, more subjective feeling in the piece of art. In music, perhaps even more than painting, there is a great deal of play in the variance which the composer has in dealing with these two elements of musical expression; thus, the examination of these two elements will help us to understand the difference between the various kind of music. For example, in rock music, there is tremendous emphasis on the individual note through electrical amplification and a tendency to extrapolate each note to the limit of the amount of energy and emotion that may be put into it. However, composition is important to the extent that a theme may be formed. The development of composition that may spring up around the theme is usually minimal. Hence, in rock music, for the most part, only the theme and the extrapolation to the utmost of the notes composing the theme have importance. Perhaps, in the future, the development of composition will appear and become more mature. Rock is a form of music that has evolved only lately and has potential to grow into a major form of music comparable to classical, baroque, and operatic.

HSKL: Of course, the emphasis and method of executing one parameter of expression more than another are not the only differences between rock and classical, or for that matter between any two kinds of music, are they?

DTMR: I'm afraid I don't understand your question yet. Can you give me an example?

HSKL: I mean, surely there are other differences – as for instance, the use of percussion in rock music, which is for the most part lacking in classical but is essential to the character of rock as a form of music.

DTMR: Yes, of course. There is not only this use of percussion that is a distinction between the two types of music. We may analyze these kinds of music and others and be able to realize the many distinctions that separate the various kinds of music and learn the components that sets them apart and gives each kind its particular uniqueness. However, all these characteristics are within the two parameters of expression and do not exist separate from them. Let's just take, as you suggested, the particular use of percussion in rock music; that is, the constant rhythmical beating that perhaps is reminiscent of rather primitive forms of music which sometimes use similar rhythmical beating patterns. Of course, the use of the percussion instrument is not just peculiar to rock as opposed to classical, as both will use that instrument to emit a certain tone, quality, etc., but it is the combination of the notes that makes the distinction. No matter what difference you may observe between forms of music, Haskell, the differences will be of one parameter or the other.

HSKL: I can see that now. You mentioned something quite interesting just now about rock and its use of the percussion being reminiscent of primitive forms of music as they have been known to also use this sort of rhythmical beating. Why would you suppose that in two different forms of music such a strong similarity as that might appear?

DTMR: Well, it's hard to say with any great certainty why exactly the similarity has evolved, but we do know for sure that each comes from artistic expression with its basis in experience. These antecedents of experiences are difficult to know as they come from within the composer, but they have a basis as actual realizations of one's own inner rhythms – such as the heartbeat, which may have been imprinted and experienced anywhere from the time the self was being formed in the womb to just before the composer is able to reach for these experiences and put them to musical expression by the rhythmical beating of a percussion instrument. When heard, it is appreciated by the listener as he also may have similar experiences locked up deep inside the self and has come to learn to recognize and assimilate (consciously or unconsciously) the patterns in the musical expression with his own self.

HSKL: Very interesting indeed. Then, music and its themes could be nothing else than the expression of biological rhythms within us, and the appreciation of music is the conscious or unconscious recognition and assimilation of such.

DTMR: Well, I would say that is a distinct possibility, but I would also add that the expression of biological rhythms most probably is not the only source from which musical expression is taken. Experience is a wide and deep reservoir where the breaths and depths are by no means clearly known, and furthermore, I must admit that even this use of the "biological rhythm" is vague and obscure and serves only to indicate the possibility of certain kinds of experiences that are suitable to be expressed musically.

HSKL: I don't follow you.

DTMR: I mean to say, Haskell, that I find it hard to realize from where and from what kind of experiences musical expression arises, and the more sublime it becomes the more impossible it becomes. The reason, I believe, is that the most sublime of music comes not from worldly, everyday, ephemeral experiences, but from deep within the complicated self, from deep within the reservoir of experience to the extent that the realizations that come forth have not any concrete form, but are abstract in the fullest sense. And perhaps, the experiences taken for musical expression run so deep as to be actual realizations of biological workings of the self, or possibly even to touch the soul.

HSKL: Thank you. I think I can understand what you are saying. The important point, however, as I see it, is that no matter how deeply a composer may delve into himself, what he uses to make his musical art is experience, whether it be a superficial, mundane experience or whether it be a realization that touches a "biological rhythm" or some other vague, obscure source of experience.

DTMR: You, obviously, understand me well, and no doubt have previously come to the same observation.

HSKL: What I would like to ask now is, how do we approach music critically? How, if we were music critics, would we approach music with our theory of music, and how would we determine what is good and bad and what is better or worse?

DTMR: Well, I believe we touched upon this before by mentioning that the standard by which one should judge music is the extent to which the composer reaches within himself and realizes the more sublime of experiences, abstracts these into his musical themes, and then proceeds to develop them to their fullest degree in his musical expression. However, if there are some points of this about which you are not clear, by all means, let us examine the problem to a full and complete extent.

HSKL: Okay. Then let us take an example. Could we apply this standard to some music and see if it can help us make some determinations and judgments concerning the various kinds of music?

DTMR: Certainly. What have you in mind?

HSKL: Well, I am not so interested in, say, whether Beethoven is a greater composer than Mozart or whether this symphony is better than that symphony. I think the present critics of music are able to deal with the subject adequately and I, for one, think that those questions are not so significant, but I am a bit interested in this question of whether rock music is actually good music and how it might fit in with other forms of music in terms of quality. I have seen learned people of music scoff at this form of music as being lowly and far from anything that has quality. Also, I am interested in whether we can by using our standard, in fact, be able to determine at all whether one form of music is inherently better than another form of music.

DTMR: Well, I think right off we may say that no discipline of music inherently, intrinsically, or essentially is better or has any more quality than another. According to what we have already postulated, the quality in the art of music lies not in the instrumentation but in the ability of the composer to abstract his experiences into musical themes and develop these to their fullest extent. The employment of instruments is only to convey the certain kinds of musical expression that the composer wishes. The guitar, the violin, or any other instrument has no inherent advantage. Hence, quality lies wholly in the author's ability to express himself musically. However, it is generally noted that some forms of music are considered to be almost, if not entirely, inferior to other forms of music. For example, it is surely almost universally thought that the quality of folk music is in general not of the level of classical, baroque, or operatic music.

HSKL: I perfectly agree so far.

DTMR: Hence, the reason that one form of music will come to be generally considered inferior to another lies in the ability of the composers of any one discipline to abstract his experiences into musical expression, and secondly, in the extent to which the composer is able to reach into himself to realize the more subtle, sublime experiences and deliver himself of these through musical expression. Thus, we may say that those composers dealing in folk music of one kind or another, in general, do not delve into themselves for musical realizations and do not abstract these into musical expression to the extent that classical, baroque, and operatic composers have done; consequently, they operate on a comparatively superficial scale. Hence, when a group of composers operates at a comparatively superficial scale, obviously, the thematic quality will not have so much of the sublime genius as with those composers that do operate on a deeper plane. If we understand this, we may soon see the reason why music enthusiasts will come to value one form of music over another form of music.

HSKL: I see. But I would like to put you in the shoes of one of these music appreciators and ask you if you could not briefly answer whether rock music is actually good music or not and how it compares to other forms of music.

DTMR: Well, as you know I prefer to leave criticism and such questions to critics and learned men who through their profession often entertain such questions. Basically, I try to stick to the questions of theory and the essence of things, but since this is an interesting question and might help to clarify our music postulation even further, let us pursue it a bit.

HSKL: Thank you.

DTMR: Rock music is by no means as steeped in quality as other forms of music, such as classical music. The great composers of classical music have abstracted the most sublime of themes and developed these in symphonies, concertos, etc.; consequently, composers like Beethoven and Mozart have exploited their themes greatly, if not to perfection. Naturally, the combination of a great theme and extensive compositional development thereof produces the apex of musical artistic expression. In rock music, we can recognize one thing immediately: the general lack of development. But rock music is young, and the lack of compositional development is to be expected. Recently, however, I believe I have begun to see some progress in this area, and if it continues, we may expect to see some rather accomplished, well-developed pieces of music arise in the rock world that may help to elevate this form of music to a sphere of greater quality. But, let me say that rock is not completely bereft of developmental quality. On the one-dimensional level of the expression of a single note, rock musicians have become adept and are fast coming to know how to deliver and exploit the single note.

HSKL: How about the quality of theme in rock music?

DTMR: Lately too I have noticed some themes of very high merit, as I mentioned before. In artists of rock music, we may find themes of such high quality that if we play them with a violin and compare them to some famous themes of classical music, we may find that some of those of rock music are just as sublime, subtle, and exalting as those of classical music. Hence, I think, though rock is young, it is rich in thematic merit and is growing and developing into an important form of music.

HSKL: Well, I am glad to hear you say so as I take an interest in rock music and like it as much as I do classical music.

DTMR: Naturally. You are young, and this music developed as you were growing up, and it is a product of the same culture and a similar set of sociological experiences. Also, it is a fervent, energetic music and moves quickly just as the young people of today do.

HSKL: Well, I believe that exhausts my questions about music and art, and except for one, I am satisfied.

DTMR: What is that? I wonder.

HSKL: Does beauty exist where there is art? For that matter, what is the connection between beauty, aesthetics, and art?

DTMR: Well now, that is a question! However, we have talked enough for one day and I for one am a bit tired and hungry. So, why don't we adjourn until tomorrow when we can take up an inquiry into beauty and aesthetics?

HSKL: Yes, that would suit me just fine. May I drop by in the morning if you are free?

DTMR: Certainly. I am always free to entertain such interesting discussions. I hope to see you tomorrow morning.

HSKL: Yes, I will certainly be here. Thank you, Detmar, and good day!

AESTHETICS

DTMR: Ah, Haskell, I am glad you could come back! Are you as well as yesterday?

HSKL: Yes, quite. Thank you. You also look well, cheerful, and rested today, Detmar.

DTMR: Thank you. I suppose you have come to continue our inquiry.

HSKL: Of course! This is interesting to me; especially since we have come to the best part – what is the place of art in aesthetics, and why is art beautiful, and is art always beauty, and if I may add, what is the nature of beauty and all of aesthetics?

DTMR: Well, perhaps we've expanded our subject, but it is just as well because we probably would have come to those questions eventually anyway.

HSKL: Yes. Of that, I am certain, as these questions have been on my mind for some time.

DTMR: Well, let us begin by proposing a definition of aesthetics and then proceed by inquiry after that. Let us suggest that aesthetics is that which pertains to beauty, and beauty is that which is recognized by man as a positive extreme.

HSKL: What? I can hardly believe the essence of beauty can be so simple. By your definition are you suggesting that when a man comes to recognize a positive extreme he necessarily comes to realize beauty and, hence, comes to realize aesthetics?

DTMR: Yes, that's correct.

HSKL: Well, then. What do you mean by the words "positive extreme?"

DTMR: By this, I mean that where there is something seen, represented, shown, or understood to have advancement, progress, achievement, or to be, otherwise, a pinnacle, apex, or culminating point in a suitable, adaptive manner to the particular situation, there will be beauty.

HSKL: I still don't understand. Maybe if we could examine an example of what you are explaining, it might become clear to me. Suppose you point out for me the positive extremes that lie in something like Yosemite Valley in Yosemite National Park, which most anyone would think, I imagine, to have beauty and to be aesthetically pleasing.

DTMR: This is an easy example, as the beauty of Yosemite is a pinnacle of the work of nature. In Yosemite, life thrives to its utmost and all is in ecological harmony; the valley and the waterfall are an apex that is of geological magnificence formed by the forces of nature. The positive extremes are, of course, seen in the workings of nature that produce such a pinnacle of life where the ecological system has come to such a height of development, and in a pinnacle of the spectacular where its novel geological forms are sculptured by nature's force. In these apexes, positive extremes are seen, and thus, beauty is perceived.

HSKL: Yes, those features of Yosemite do seem to be, as you say, positive extremes. Let's take another example. What about something like a single mountain such as Mount Ranier in Washington or Mount Fuji in Japan? The sight of these mountains is certainly beautiful. In Japan Mount Fuji is pictured everywhere to the point of being worshipped. How is the sight of these mountains beautiful?

DTMR: Well, your example is similar to Yosemite. The beauty of the mountains lies in the spectacular forces of nature that were necessary to produce such stirring feats of geological consequence.

HSKL: But in this case, especially concerning Mount Fuji, the form itself is important. If Mount Fuji were just as large but its outline against the horizon was not as regular and symmetrical, it might not be so beautiful. It seems that some of the beauty of the mountains lies in the form of the mountains themselves.

DTMR: Yes, you are right. But still, the form is beautiful if we recognize the tremendous volcanic forces of nature that were necessary to give rise to Mount Fuji and Mount Ranier and give them such a symmetrical form. But if you were to, without notion and thought of or without any reference to these two peaks, draw an outline on a piece of paper similar to the outline of these mountains, the outline on the paper would not appear particularly aesthetically pleasing or displeasing. One would simply see a symmetrical form on a piece of paper and attach no special aesthetic significance to it whatsoever. However, if you were to see this outline on the piece of paper in terms of its relation to the configuration of Mount Fuji or Mount Ranier, and were to rethink the figure in this light, you would immediately attach aesthetical significance to the form and come to think of the symmetrical figure as pleasing. Hence, we may say that the positive extreme of nature that was capable of producing something so spectacularly domineering of its surroundings and comparatively representative of forces that could carve such a clear, clean figure of such momentous size from the earth is certainly an extreme, and therein lies the beauty of the mountains.

HSKL: How is it that you think those forces positive? In my mind, I would not think them either positive or negative; they just exist.

DTMR: Yes, if you perceive or interpret these forces as simply existing with no positive or negative value, then you will view the mountain as simply existing and hence you will not be able to recognize the beauty that is of Mount Fuji or Mount Ranier. Simply, you would view them and they would not occasion any particular response within you. However, should you realize that the forces behind the making of the mountains were part of those terrific forces of nature that gave life to the earth, and should you recognize that without the energy that gives rise to such momentous consequences life itself could not be, then you would certainly place a positive value upon this extreme.

HSKL: However, people do not see beauty in terms of the positiveness of nature's energy. They do not look at an object of beauty and know the positiveness of the object, especially if the persons are uneducated and do not know the specific workings of nature that are involved. If a person is not educated and cannot recognize that the positiveness of the beauty of something originates itself in the energies of nature, how can he know and understand that something is beautiful?

DTMR: He can by his aesthetic sense. If he has developed his aesthetic sense, he will become aware of the beauty of an object which has a positive extreme. This aesthetic sense of his will ferret out the positive extreme and he will sense its beauty. Of course, his self does this in an unconscious way, and he does not say to himself when contemplating an object of beauty, "Oh, there is positive extreme there; therefore, I recognize the beauty involved and I feel aesthetically impressed." No, obviously, this does not happen, and one does not need to analyze in such a way to feel and know beauty. There is a faculty within the self that promotes the sensing of the aesthetic, and the analysis of this is the subject of the present conversation.

HSKL: Of course. Well, let's just backtrack a bit. I would like to know if I have things straight so far. Now, if I understand you correctly, if we perceive things that are considered general in nature to be beautiful and recognize that these are positive extremes in nature, then we will perceive that they are beautiful. Also, if we recognize that the positiveness of the beauty originates itself in the energies of nature, which provide the energies for that particular beautiful thing and, in fact, provide for all of life, then we will realize its positiveness and therefore its beauty.

DTMR: That is correct.

HSKL: Well, might I suggest that the positive energy that provides for a thing of beauty like Yosemite or Mount Fuji is also the same energy that provides the opportunity or the means for things in nature that are not generally considered beautiful, such as a mosquito or a parasite. Such things are certainly not considered beautiful, yet as you say, a positive energy supports them. I still am not convinced that this energy can be considered either positive or negative; in the case of a parasite, it supports something not so beautiful, but on the other hand, it is the same force that you call the positive force of Yosemite. Therefore, in that it can cause and maintain things both beautiful and not beautiful, and can even support and maintain things that can be considered actually ugly, I cannot see how these forces of nature or the universe can be construed to be either positive or negative.

DTMR: Good point, Haskell. I believe the answer to this lies in the understanding that, on the surface, a mosquito or a parasite is not beautiful to look at nor the thought of them pleasant, but if we were to view them as an integral part of the whole, where they serve a purpose and have come into a place where they operate and exist according to certain limitations and pressures, then I think we may begin to see that there is a positive side to their existence made possible by the input of positive energy.

HSKL: I don't follow you yet. What is this positive side of parasites that you speak of?

DTMR: I am saying that indeed if you look upon the parasite and such like beings superficially, we can only see something that has no aesthetic association about it. However, if we consider that each animal has come to find a niche in nature and is an integral and requisite part in the whole structure and that there is an energy, a force, that caused parameters to construct limitations and pressures that came to bear upon life and produced the appearance of something like a mosquito or a fly or a parasite, then we can begin to understand the aesthetic side of something even as insignificant as the lower forms of life. Let me emphasize also that the appearance of all these kinds of life is requisite and integral to the whole and each has its purpose with its own select pressures operating upon it. Hence, in the context of a life's own particular purpose, that kind of life, such as that of a fly, extends itself to its utmost, and within its own sphere of purpose, it is an extreme, and in the realization of an extreme and in the realization of the whole which supports man himself at the pinnacle, is a positive extreme; thus, there can be appreciated an aesthetic point of view of even the lower forms of life. If one just looks at a mosquito flying around a room, then one would not be imbued with any sense of beauty; however, if that person looks upon the mosquito in the light of an integral part of the entire scheme of nature, residing in its certain niche, then that person may be imbued with a feeling of aesthetic quality through this particular point of view.

HSKL: I see. As I gather it, beauty can be found where there is a positive extreme, and when considering the scheme of life, not only can beauty be found in obvious extremes of life, as for example, in man himself, but in base, mean forms of life also. If a lower form of life is viewed as serving the whole in a certain capacity or in a specific way, the lower form of life takes on a small importance all its own particular to itself and is in its own way an extreme, and in view of the integral and requisite part that it plays in the workings of nature, we may find that there is a characteristic parameter in its position within the total structure of things that we may deem to be a positive extreme. Hence, there may be found some beauty within its situation, although its quantity and intensity of beauty may not be as great as that of higher forms.

DTMR: I see you understand me perfectly.

HSKL: Yes, so far so good. I can see the beauty of the lower form of life, but only in that it is an integral part of the great beautiful whole of nature. This I can understand. But do these lower products of nature hold the same force or impact of beauty as the beauty of a higher form of life? For example, does an insect hold the same amount of beauty as does the majestic lion, the sleek leopard, the muscular Arabian stallion, or any other superb examples from the animal world?

DTMR: No. In general, the lower forms of life do not impart as deep an impact of beauty as the higher forms of life. Obviously, an Arabian horse is understandably thought to be of greater aesthetic value than a snail or an insect, or most forms of lower life. And this is so because the Arabian horse or most other higher forms of animal life are, obviously, higher forms and examples of the positive extreme. Nature had to work a great deal harder to produce these higher forms of life, and hence they are of an obvious greater positive extreme; therefore, I'm sure we may assert without much argument the greater aesthetic value of the Arabian stallion.

HSKL: Right. I am in agreement about seeing the greater intensity of beauty of an Arabian stallion or any other higher form of life over something of the lower forms of life such as a snail, fly, or mosquito. However, you said, Detmar, "in general" this is so. Why did you use those words as opposed to "in every case"? Are there any exceptions to this rule?

DTMR: Yes, we must say "in general" because, although I would not say there are "exceptions," there are some cases where a lower form of life has become so much a pinnacle or an apex in its own right or in its own little slot of nature that the intensity of its beauty is startling and extreme and shows itself to be a positive extreme of great magnitude.

HSKL: Of what do you speak?

DTMR: I speak of the most beautiful butterflies, or the most fascinating tropical fish, and other such examples. A most striking butterfly does not have the grandeur and awesomeness of the beauty of the leopard, lion, or horse, but it does have a fascinating, startling appeal in its beauty that is not easily found anywhere in nature. Now, perhaps overall we really cannot put the beauty of a butterfly or a tropical fish on the same level as that of a thoroughbred horse since the grandeur, scale, and size of the horse are so much greater, but within the frame of its natural place or niche, the butterfly can excel to great lengths and present a positive extreme that will exhibit an intense and extreme form of beauty. Hence, within its own frame of positiveness, the butterfly, or the tropical fish, or whatever can present a unique aesthetic value that can be of tremendous intensity and extremity.

HSKL: If that is so, then are we able to compare beauties and inquire whether one thing is more beautiful than another thing?

DTMR: Yes, we can. But when we make a comparison, we must keep in mind a certain frame of aesthetic sense. When we appreciate and weigh the beauties of our butterfly and our Arabian stallion, in overall scope and scale of aesthetic impact there is a clear advantage with the horse. It fits high in the animal kingdom, and again the range, scope, and extent of its positive extremes provide an impact of aesthetic intensity that is in its entirety much greater than that of the butterfly. However, note that I maintain that in the entirety and scope of its positive extremes, its beauty is greater. I say that because there is a frame of aesthetic sense and awareness one must have in mind when making a comparison or contrast between the aesthetic impact of one thing and another. This frame of aesthetic sense refers to the awareness that, although the scope and range of the beauty of the Arabian stallion may provide a greater impact on the impression of beauty, and although the beauty of a butterfly is limited in grandeur, the butterfly can have an intensity of beauty evolving from its particular niche that it fills all alone, and thus, produces an aesthetic impression that is commensurate with the extent to which it has become a positive extreme. Hence, the Monarch butterfly can give a particular, singular type of an intense impression of beauty that is particular to itself alone and perhaps unmatchable by anything in the realm of nature, but it cannot give the scope of composite beauty that the grandeur of the Arabian horse can.

HSKL: I don't wholly follow you. What do you mean by composite beauty?

DTMR: Well, if we take our former example of Yosemite and compare the beauty of that with a monarch butterfly (that may even perhaps live in Yosemite) and put it alongside the total composite beauty of Yosemite, then one can quickly see that the singular beauty of the butterfly, although intense in itself, is not the spectacular, vast beauty of the whole of Yosemite. Even though there is a whole spectacular beauty of Yosemite, if dissected, there are integral parts of aesthetic value that make the whole and give the whole its scope and range of beauty.

HSKL: I see. Well, let's return to where we were before. We postulated that there is a positiveness about beauty. Also, we have postulated that when the extent to which the positiveness is realized in whatever direction it proceeds, then one may understand the aesthetics of the thing in question. However, I am not quite sure where the beauty lies: does it lie in the thing being observed or in, as the old adage says, "the eye of the beholder," meaning that beauty varies with the person? As you know, one person will consider one thing beautiful, and the next person will not hold the thing in any sort of aesthetic awe whatsoever.

DTMR: As everyone has different powers of perception, obviously, there will be differences in the way people will view something, and naturally various interpretations will be made regarding the aesthetics of any one thing, but the ideal of beauty, or the nature and essence of beauty, is uniform and in every case, it is a positive extreme. The knowledge or feeling of this positive extreme is the aesthetic sense, and anybody who has an aesthetic sense and can feel and know beauty is instilled with this capacity of sensing the positive extreme. Hence, when the person who enjoys the aesthetic contemplates something of beauty, he becomes aware of the beauty by perceiving the positive extreme in the thing; he is contemplating and matching this with his own conception and perception of the positive extreme which lies within him. If he can find outside of him that which accords with his feeling of the positive extreme that lies within him, then he will find beauty. Therefore, the reason why two people will declare different opinions concerning the beauty of any one thing which they may be contemplating lies in their ability to perceive the positive extremes about the thing they consider. They have within them a sense of the positive extreme, and when they can perceive this they are recognizing what is called beauty or aesthetics. This perception of the positive extreme is nothing else but the sense of aesthetics.

HSKL: Well, as I understand it, there has been imbued into man this aesthetic sense, which is none other than the sense of positive extremes. Then, when a person seeks that which is beautiful, he looks to the world and from his sense of aesthetics extrapolates that which is beautiful from that which he is contemplating. Thus, our old adage is not entirely correct as the qualities and attributes that make something essentially and actually beautiful lie in the thing being observed, but the perception and conception of whether something is beautiful or not lies in him who is observing the thing.

DTMR: Yes, and the observer must undergo the process of extrapolating his sense of beauty (which, as we must take it, is nothing else but an interior-originating experience) to what he sees (an exterior-originating experience) and then come to a realization concerning the state of aesthetics involved in the thing being observed. Hence, it might be understood that this operation is no different from what the artist uses before he begins to express himself. The observer of the aesthetic is undergoing the operation that allows him to construct his own personal views of the world through experience, which in this case is the view of aesthetics. Through his extrapolation, he will perceive beauty in his own specific way and would become an artist if he were to express how he perceives the aesthetic.

HSKL: That's very interesting, how aesthetics and art are related. But to return to my question of whether beauty lies in the eyes of the beholder or not, the answer seems to be that beauty lies in the perception of whether something is a positive extreme or not. That is, beauty lies in the assimilation of an exterior-originating experience and in determining whether or not this experience fits the certain parameters of the notion of the positive extreme. Hence, beauty lies in the ability to perceive the positive extreme.

DTMR: That's, absolutely, correct. I see you comprehend this matter completely.

HSKL: Thank you. I believe I understand for the most part what we have covered so far, but something that was just said a minute ago has set me thinking a bit.

DTMR: How so?

HSKL: As you know, Detmar, my interests are not exclusively philosophically oriented. I have a strong background in science, and I know you are aware that many scientists have a great interest in philosophy. Possibly somewhere these disciplines of science and philosophy meet and become the same.

DTMR: Yes, I understand what you are saying.

HSKL: We, just a bit ago, postulated that people who feel beauty are imbued with a sense of the aesthetic, or more precisely, are imbued with a sense of the positive extreme. If I could know its origin and why and how it came to be, I would be more sure of my comprehension of these matters we have been discussing today.

DTMR: As I understand it, you would like to know the reason for the aesthetic sense in mankind. HSKL: Yes, that's correct.

DTMR: And this would help you assure yourself that we are following the right lines in our inquiry into the essence of beauty.

HSKL: Yes, it would most assuredly.

DTMR: Haskell, I gather you are well acquainted with biology and anthropology.

HSKL: I have studied biology and some anthropology.

DTMR: Then you are aware of how natural selection works?

HSKL: Yes, of course.

DTMR: Well, then. I would like to suggest to you that the origin of the aesthetic sense and the reason for this sense of appreciating beauty evolved in mankind simply because it proved to be adaptive; it helped him survive in his environment.

HSKL: How so? How could a sense of positive extreme possibly have been an adaptive factor in man's evolution? What good would it have done to have developed this sense in man's everyday struggle for survival, and how did this sense help to enable man to adapt to his environment in the course of evolution? Also, why did not other species evolve this sense?

DTMR: To begin with, no other species developed the aesthetic sense because it evolved in conjunction with the evolution of culture. Often in the evolution of man, the genetic side has influenced the evolution of culture, and likewise, the evolution of culture has much influenced the genetic evolution of man. I believe most biologists and physical anthropologists would agree here.

HSKL: It certainly would seem reasonable.

DTMR: The aesthetic sense evolved because it helped provide the ability in man to recognize, regard, and maintain that which is useful and adaptive. For example, a simple tool becomes appreciated by its user when he sees it is a good one. The more the certain tool is refined and perfected (and thereby becomes a positive extreme) for the purpose for which it is made, the more it takes on beauty. We often hear men who use a certain tool and are aware of its uses say that the particular tool is beautiful and they openly appreciate it. This is because the particular tool is one of the best ones available and its use is great. A good instance of this line of thinking is men's attitude toward and appreciation of a knife. Often men who use a particular knife, appreciate it and praise the knife to no end when they believe it is of great service to them and when they clearly recognize its functional use. The more the knife is functional, the more their appreciation of it grows.

HSKL: Is this appreciation of which you speak aesthetic appreciation?

DTMR: Yes, of course. This appreciation derives itself from the roots of aesthetic appreciation and is no different. Let's examine the case of a gun. This is a more refined and complicated tool than the knife. It can be used in obtaining food, in self-defense, or in aggression. The more a gun becomes dependable, accurate, and useful and the more it has been refined for these purposes, the more the user through his aesthetic sense will recognize the gun's function and the extent to which it has been developed; he then becomes appreciative of it, admires it, and may even put it on display. Obviously, he likes the sight of the gun and appreciates it for the positive extremes about it; that is, he admires the gun for its beauty. Often, Haskell, one hears the expressions "It's a beauty," "Isn't it beautiful?" or "Isn't it a beauty?" The aesthetic sense is working here to produce such a reaction to the tool. The more the tool is useful (and therefore adaptive), the more it will inspire admiration in its user; that is, the more the tool follows a positive extreme, the more it will inspire aesthetic appreciation.

HSKL: But how does this aesthetic appreciation of a tool or anything else have an adaptive advantage for man?

DTMR: It is because this sense helps to recognize and maintain functional things. If one recognizes the functions of something and appreciates it, then that someone will maintain it and preserve it. This has definitely an adaptive advantage in evolutionary terms and would soon be incorporated into the genetic and/or cultural machinery of man by natural selection.

HSKL: I see. What you are purporting here basically is that of the old adage: form follows function. Form that follows function will necessarily take on an aesthetic appeal, and hence, aspects of beauty will be found within.

DTMR: That's correct, although it does not tell the whole story.

HSKL: Well, I can't see how the adage that form follows function can be the rule of beauty. It seems to me that there are many exceptions to this.

DTMR: Let's examine some and see.

HSKL: What about a plain old machine or a tractor or one of these giant earth-moving trucks? These, it seems to me, are extremely functional, yet where is the beauty to be found?

DTMR: You are not an engineer and cannot know how the machine works; you do not know the extent to which the machine has been refined and do not know its capabilities; you cannot truly recognize the workings and functional capacities. Thus, you cannot appreciate the machine. An engineer, however, who is fully acquainted with a particular piece of equipment may recognize that the piece has a marvelous engineering design, has tremendous capacities, and is well constructed, and thus, will appreciate the machine and may think it to be, in its particular, specific frame of the aesthetic, beautiful. The engineer will think in terms of a "beautiful design," "superb construction," etc. He, obviously, sees it in a different manner than you, Haskell.

HSKL: Yes, I suppose he would. What did you mean when you said "particular, specific frame of the aesthetic"?

DTMR: Each object of beauty has to be viewed in its particular frame of aesthetic reference in order to appreciate it fully. For example, just now you declared that you could not see the beauty inherent in a large earth-moving machine.

HSKL: Yes.

DTMR: This is only because you were viewing this huge tractor not on its own terms. Perhaps you were viewing it in terms of a vehicle that goes fast. The point is that you must view the great earth-moving tractor on its ability to fulfill the purpose for which it was built and to the extent that that tractor goes to a positive extreme in fulfilling that purpose. If the purpose is not that extensive, then the positive extreme will not be so extensive or extreme; hence, there will not be found so much beauty.

However, if the purpose is extensive and the positive extreme is there and the particular thing (in this case it is our earthmoving tractor) fulfills its purpose, then it will have the property of being in the positive extreme and we will find beauty there.

HSKL: How does this answer my question? It's unclear yet.

DTMR: The frame of aesthetical reference is the particular positive extreme that the thing (or object) of beauty follows and tries to fulfill. Thus, if one does not recognize the specific direction of the positive extreme or specific purpose to which the thing lends itself or the singular functional niche which it holds, then one cannot know the extent of the beauty that lies therein. As we have already postulated, the extent of beauty is the degree of the positive extreme, and how extreme this positiveness runs, and also the scope and range of its positiveness (as we say with the comparison of the beauties of the monarch butterfly and the Arabian stallion) determine the particular aesthetic frame for which one must search in order to know the beauty of any one thing.

HSKL: I believe I'm beginning to get the picture. In regard to my viewing the earth-mover, I could not comprehend its aesthetic qualities as I was not using my sight in a suitable way to determine the extreme to which it is positive; I was not recognizing the specific purpose of the machine and how well this machine fulfilled that purpose. As you say, if I were an engineer, I would be better able to look at the earth-mover and see, understand, and appreciate its aesthetic points.

DTMR: Right. Of course, the particular tractor or machine may not have many pleasing aesthetical points, depending on how well it can carry out its function and how great that function is. If it does not have a positiveness to it, it cannot have beauty, and if it does not take that positiveness to any extreme, then it will not have very much beauty. If our particular earth-mover is a stirring example of engineering, then it will have beauty because it will be the manifestation of some brilliant engineering minds. Also, these minds are in themselves positive extremes, and when they produce something that requires their full capacity, then that finished thing will also have aesthetic qualities because it will also be of a positive extreme. I for one am not an engineer and not able to quickly discern the intricacies inherent in engineering; so like you, I might not see the singular aesthetic qualities of an earth-mover, but that does not mean there are none. The best judge of how far a particular machine moves in a positive extreme would of course be an engineer.

HSKL: Yes, I wholly agree now. However, there are still some problems in my mind as to this form-follows-function adage.

DTMR: Yes?

HSKL: I believe I'm coming to understand and agree with you about the essence of beauty being of the positive extreme, but unfortunately, I'm still a bit skeptical about this adage that everything that is beautiful has to follow function. I think, though, I can see that everything that has function has to have some beauty.

DTMR: Let me interrupt a second, Haskell. I do not believe we can say that where there is function beauty will necessarily follow. Let's not lose sight of the essence of aesthetics: that beauty lies in the positive extreme. In some very crude and yet functional items, we find not much beauty. We find the beauty in an extreme of that function, in refinement, in extrapolation, in cultivation of a functional thing. It must be a pinnacle, a climax, a culminating point to know appreciable beauty.

HSKL: Is that to say there can be no beauty in something very crude yet very functional?

DTMR: If it is in all aspects crude, then it will be devoid of aesthetic qualities. However, one must be careful in order to know that something is truly devoid of beauty, as one must be able to consider all the frames of aesthetical reference. For example, if I contemplate a simple shovel, I feel no stirrings of aesthetical pleasure within me, yet this tool is functional. However, if we were to think that perhaps three million years ago some man or some near ancestor of man through the genius and inventiveness of the species produced the first shovel not too much unlike the one presently being contemplated, then the situation seems to take on a certain aspect of aesthetic quality. The origin of this aesthetic quality derives itself from a different, obscure frame of aesthetic reference: the shovel, albeit crude, is an embodiment of the genius and inventiveness of man as a whole and as a species.

HSKL: I see, but the inventiveness of man is the beautiful part, not the shovel.

DTMR: Yes, of course. If you completely divorce the crude shovel from inventiveness, then that tool loses its aesthetic qualities. Once they became easy to make, and once better and more efficient tools were produced, then our regular shovel fades in aesthetic significance. But there is an aspect of aesthetic quality that one may attach to it and that quality lies in its origins.

HSKL: Okay. Let's get back to another question I had.

DTMR: Certainly.

HSKL: I am wondering whether all form has function; that is, whether that which is beautiful has to have function. By what we have postulated so far it would seem that it would, yet I can think of some examples where I would be hard-pressed to see functional usage. Modern art and beauties of nature such as the Grand Canyon and the Grand Tetons would be a couple of good examples.

DTMR: Good question, Haskell. You're right, to relate all forms to function would be difficult, but let's again not lose sight of the reason for the appearance of the aesthetic sense in man – to help man adapt to his environment. Something may not have to be directly usable in some basic activity as a spear is for hunting; there may have been more subtle ways developed by natural selection that helped man to adapt. Let's take some of your examples and see if we can come to a better understanding of the problem.

HSKL: Fine. Let's take modern art. In some of the works of sculpture or paintings where the abstraction is so great, the relation between the reason for beauty, adaptability, and the beauty of the abstract forms created by the artist is quite beyond me.

DTMR: We covered this problem a bit a short while ago, but let's try and clear a few things up by recapitulating some of our basic postulations. First, we know the reason for the appearance of the aesthetic sense in man: first, it came to be that a recognition of that which is adaptive is adaptive in itself; second, the essence of beauty lies in that it is a positive extreme, and the recognition of this positive extreme is adaptive. I believe you have some examples that have a positive extreme, but you cannot understand how they are adaptive. One of your examples is modern art. As you are probably thinking, man surely did not have to have modern art to survive these past three or four million years or so.

HSKL: Yes, the problem of modern art is certainly one of them.

DTMR: Well, I think if we determine first how something is beautiful, or how something is a positive extreme, we will be able to see the relationship.

HSKL: Fine.

DTMR: With art, the beauty (the positive extreme) lies in how well and to what extent the author is able to express how he sees the world. Art, as we have already postulated, is the expression of how the artist sees his world; the extent to which he does this will determine its beauty. If the extent runs to an extreme, beauty will become intense. The positiveness of art clearly is that it teaches us about our world around us, about how we ourselves think, how those around us think and act. It teaches and explores human nature and what constitutes our makeup. It is, obviously, positive. Thus, when an artist does his job well, his work takes on a positive extreme and hence takes on the quality of beauty, because art is positive and good art is an extreme in that it is the pinnacle of expression of how one sees the world.

HSKL: I see. But I still don't see the utility of something like the forms presented in modern sculpture. I still cannot see either their basic functional good, why they would be adaptive, or their positiveness.

DTMR: That's because you're not putting yourself in the proper aesthetic perspective. These forms are not functional tools for physical labor like a shovel is; they are intellectually functional. They are positive extremes in that (when done well) they are spectacular expressions of how the artist sees the world (which is art). And if we remember that previously we decided there is obvious value in art, then we may soon see the obvious positiveness about the expressiveness in art.

HSKL: I understand now. Also, I can see that when we can determine the positiveness of something, we will be able to establish that something will have a function, usage, or adaptability of some sort inherent in it (which will constitute the positiveness of it). Also, I understand that in order to realize the nature of aesthetics, we must first recognize its positiveness and then its extent of positiveness.

DTMR: That's right.

HSKL: However, there are still some problems that remain for me in determining the aesthetic positiveness of things.

DTMR: What are those problems?

HSKL: Most people who go to Switzerland and view the scenic mountains and lovely valleys are filled with aesthetic appreciation and exclaim how beautiful the land is. I wondered if you could explain to me how the landscape of Switzerland would be beautiful. But before you begin, I would like to declare that I believe that a Swiss of yore who lived in one of those small, serene hamlets that everybody considers so beautiful – who had to toil every day in those valleys for his living and had to endure walking the high, steep roads and the hardships of trekking through the mountain passes – would not think of the land as beautiful. Through his heavy toil, he would not associate his surroundings with that which is aesthetic. Also, in the same vein, I would surmise that a poor farmer who toils on his land day in and day out growing his crops and undergoing his hard lifestyle would not consider the place he lives beautiful. Yet I know that when people not associated with the area go to Ireland and view the countryside, they are filled with aesthetic admiration and declare how beautiful it all is. Why are there two opinions here?

How can something be both beautiful and not beautiful at the same time?

DTMR: That is a good question, Haskell, but I think the answer lies in something we discussed a little while ago. The reason for the two different interpretations of the same thing is because the aesthetic frame of reference is not the same. The Swiss and the farmer when they are striving in their land may see their surroundings in light of struggle or toil and not in a positive way. Hence, if they do not contemplate a positiveness and the extent or extremity of the positiveness, they will not perceive the beauty. However, someone not associated with their struggles will take a different referential approach and recognize a positiveness of the land and the extent of its positiveness. Someone not associated with the struggles of the land will see the green fertile valleys and the high peaks of the Alps and naturally will immediately recognize the positive extremes there. Someone not acquainted with the toils of the farmer will look upon the verdure of the countryside and be filled with a sense of aesthetic admiration. But also, if the Swiss or the farmer were to take a bit of time away from his toils, which he will be able to do if there is a positive agricultural (and/or some other) extremity, sit back, and forget certain toils for a second and look upon the positive side of this life and surroundings, then he also will begin to see the beauty of his land.

HSKL: I see. Could you further explain how the Swiss and other bucolic countrysides would be considered beautiful?

DTMR: Anytime we analyze beauty we must have in mind our postulation of the positive extreme. If we view a Swiss hamlet among the peaks of the Alps, we notice the positiveness that the village is neat, clean, orderly, the buildings are well constructed and well maintained, and there seems to be little or no poverty.

The hamlet is surrounded by green fields (if it's spring or summer) that look fertile and support the town, so it appears to be enjoying adequate prosperity. So far all these things have a positiveness about them that is reasonably extensive. Obviously, people have adjusted well there in their little niche among the mountains. Viewing this, one will be struck with aesthetic wonder. In addition to the surrounding fields, there is a spectacular geological extremity that is a magnificent manifestation of the natural forces within the earth and the universe. The forces at work there, as we discussed earlier, are positive and hence, hold aesthetic qualities.

HSKL: Thank you. I'm definitely coming to realize the nature of aesthetics now through the supportive understanding of these examples.

DTMR: I'm glad to hear that. Are there any places yet that you don't clearly understand that we can explore?

HSKL: There are only a couple of things still.

DTMR: By all means, please.

HSKL: The other day I went to a museum showing of American quilt designs. Displayed were quilts with fabulous colors arranged in various unique and often very complicated geometric designs. I was wondering why it is that these geometric designs were valued and considered to have aesthetic value. I felt myself that they did have aesthetic value and that they were beautiful, but I couldn't analyze why.

DTMR: Indeed, Haskell, geometric designs can have beauty in certain contexts. If you understand the thought, the work, and the time that the maker of one of those quilts had to undergo and the extremity of ability that was employed in conceiving the geometric design, color patterns of individual patches, and the skill of sewing inherent in the final product, then we can realize the essence of its beauty. We must see and realize the positive extremes inherent in the thing of aesthetic quality if we are trying to analyze its beauty.

HSKL: I agree. One final question.

DTMR: Yes?

HSKL: What we have been discussing these past few days has been, I believe, philosophical in nature. This brings to mind one final problem: in summary what is the difference between philosophy, literature, and art? Which is more inclusive? I remember at the beginning of our inquiry we dealt briefly with the subject of philosophy being literature but perhaps we could go over it again.

DTMR: In order to answer this, I think the first thing to do is recall our definitions. First, art is the expression of how one sees the world (using both interior- and exterior-originating experiences); secondly, literature is the written expression of how one sees the world. Thus, we know that art is inclusive of literature. As to philosophy, would you say that it is inclusive of literature, separate from literature, outside the realm of both literature and art, or of literature and/or art?

HSKL: In the past, under the influence of my teachers, I would have said that philosophy was all-inclusive and contained not only all of literature and art but also all the disciplines.

DTMR: And now? Now, what do you think?

HSKL: In the past couple of days, I have come to think differently. If literature, as we have postulated, is the written expression of how one sees the world using both interior- and exterior-originating experiences, then literature should be inclusive of philosophy as well, I feel.

DTMR: Why?

HSKL: Philosophy, it would seem to me, is also an expression of how one sees the world.

DTMR: Excellent, Haskell, excellent. You have not let the past philosophical miseducation by your teachers stifle your present creative thinking.

HSKL: Yes, sir.

DTMR: Philosophy is of literature, as you so correctly deduced.

HSKL: But how is it of literature? Certainly, all literature is not philosophy. When would literature be philosophy and not philosophy?

DTMR: Most literature is not normally considered philosophical, but do not people who know literature well often speak of most works in philosophical terms when talking about the essence of a particular work?

HSKL: What do you mean?

DTMR: We often hear, when listening to people discussing great works of literature, such topics as man versus nature, man's place in the universe, man's identity, or how about faith, God, love, virtue, morals, etc.? All these subjects smack of a philosophical connotation, yet they are all found in literature. I think it would be hard not to purport that all (at least good) literature has some elements of philosophy in it.

HSKL: Yes, I agree. When it comes to good literature, and not the dime novel of the drugstore genre, its core very often seems to hold some aspect of a philosophical nature. But still, I maintain that most good literary works essentially are not philosophical and seem different from the works of Plato, Descartes, Berkeley, etc. They seem for the most part philosophical, yet still purport to show how one sees the world, which makes them, basically, works of literature. Under our definitions so far, philosophy should be of literature, yet I feel they are separate.

DTMR: All philosophy is literary art, and all literary art holds at least some grain of philosophical essence. Philosophy being one kind of literary art, it is one kind of expression of how the artist sees the world. The kind of literature that we would consider philosophy deals with, for the most part, inner-originating experiences; literary art deals with, for the most part, exterior-originating experiences. Let me emphasize before you unleash your barrage of questions that I say "for the most part" because, obviously, there are works that are right in the middle between philosophy and literary art, such as works of Camus and Sartre that are heavily philosophical, yet written in a literary, artistic vein.

HSKL: I don't quite understand yet. How does philosophy deal mainly in-interior-originating experiences and literature in exterior-originating ones?

DTMR: Philosophy deals with the nature of concepts and how one views, realizes, and interprets those concepts, and concepts are experiences of the inner self. Of course, they are influenced from the exterior-originating experiences, but concepts are experiences in response to the exterior of the self that originate and come from within the self. Literature deals with the experience of the self undergoing interaction with the world, and hence, the majority of experiences that are employed in literary art are of the exterior kind, but of course, the interior-originating experiences are also copiously utilized. However, the more they are employed and the more they become central to the work, then the more that work of literary art will take on a philosophical air.

HSKL: Doesn't philosophy deal considerably with exterior-originating experiences?

DTMR: Yes, certainly. But the main issues, subjects, or themes of work and much of the experience expressed in the work will be interior-originating experiences when the work is basically philosophical in nature.

HSKL: I'm not completely sure I understand all this.

DTMR: Let's take an example. Let's examine Descartes' famous *Meditations*. This is a very philosophical work, you would agree?

HSKL: Certainly.

DTMR: Let's look at where Descartes begins in his meditations. He first tries to vanquish all exterior-originating experiences, and when he does, he is able to find a starting point for constructing his way of looking at the world. But nowhere is his work as philosophical as at the beginning, and when he comes to know his famous realization of "I think, therefore I am." Here is the starting point, the core of his knowledge, and it deals with wholly interior-originating experiences. From there he builds upon his knowledge, incorporating and considering other experiences, both interior- and exterior-originating ones. But the work remains philosophical because its subject is interior-originating concerns, and it deals with these extensively throughout the work.

HSKL: I'm beginning to understand, I think. Perhaps, you could take an example of a work that is considered to be philosophical but also is thought to be a work of literature. Say, for instance, Camus' *The Stranger*.

DTMR: First of all, don't forget that philosophy is of literary art. But let me put forth also that philosophy and literature can be, by and large, divided into two sub-disciplines of literary art. Thus, we may say that both are kinds of literary art.

HSKL: Fine.

DTMR: Central to Camus' *The Stranger* are some interior-originating experiences, but the manner in which these are dealt, explained, and examined are with exterior-originating experiences. Camus deals with Meursault's thoughts of happiness and what makes his existence comfortable, and the thematic core of the novel is concerned with the interior-originating experiences of Meursault, but the novel does not just stay there. It goes in and out of the use of Meursault's inner-originating experiences and employs exterior ones also to help show what kind of man Meursault is. The novel follows Meursault to his office, to the sea, to a courtroom, and to a prison. It is clear the use of both interior and exterior is widely employed; thus, the novel takes on both the aspects of a philosophical work and of literature.

HSKL: It would seem to me, reflecting a bit on the subject, that one of the major differences between philosophy and literature is that philosophy employs a great deal of logic in developing its theme whereas literature does not.

DTMR: A very good point, Haskell, Excellent. That is a difference, and one that is very important because logic is one of those interior-originating experiences that is widely present throughout important philosophical works and is not used as extensively in literature. Its use is a major difference between philosophy and literature, but remember, it is not the only difference as it is but one interior-originating experience, though one that is employed extensively in philosophical works.

HSKL: Then logic is representative of the essence of the difference between philosophy and literature as logic is an example of an interior-originating experience.

DTMR: That's correct.

HSKL: What about works of literature that are not considered philosophical at all? Are there elements of the philosophical in them or are they strictly and entirely literature?

DTMR: Are you speaking of authors such as Dickens, Shakespeare, Wordsworth, Twain, and all the other great literary artists?

HSKL: Yes, concerning famous works of literature, are they purely works of literature or are they also philosophical?

DTMR: Of course, they are basically works of literature; however, they do contain inner originating experiences, and at this point they take on a philosophical tinge. Shakespearean works are often thought to have philosophical ramifications. This is because central to each work there will be an inner originating experience that will be developed extensively but usually by the exterior-originating experiences of actions by the character. However, this is not always the case. Often in

Shakespeare, the character will express further his inner originating experiences.

HSKL: And that is why Shakespeare's plays or any other parts of literature take on philosophical hues: the development of interior-originating experiences.

DTMR: That's correct. Poetry often has philosophical ramifications as it often deals heavily with the interaction of inner and exterior experiences. Frequently in poetry, there is an exterior experience that is delineated, and then the reaction of the poet (an interior-originating experience) is expressed and is central to the work. Hence, poems often take on quite a philosophical bent. There are some poems that are considered literature but venture into the areas of philosophy extensively by the amount of interior-originating experiences employed. A good example here is the *Essay on Man* by Alexander Pope. Pope uses his interior-originating experiences concerning a specific subject, and examining the poem, one can see Pope thinking through those matters upon which he writes. Thus, although the poem is generally considered to be literary art, it is also considered to be significantly philosophically concerned.

To summarize, Haskell, all philosophy is of literary art and all literary art contains elements of the philosophical. However, the more a piece of literary art concerns itself with interior-originating experiences, the more it can be considered to be of the philosophical and thus, we can say, of philosophical literary art.

HSKL: I believe I can begin to understand clearly the difference between philosophy and literature. There is one more question about philosophy I would like to ask you.

DTMR: I say this in a complimentary way, Haskell: with you, there is always another question.

HSKL: What is the difference between philosophy and religion? It is often said that the Bible is a great work of literature and I believe it is so, but how is it different from philosophy?

DTMR: There again, a good question.

HSKL: Thank you.

DTMR: The Bible is literature as it relates things according to how the authors assimilated the world, and as you already have realized, all philosophy is literary art. Thus, we must distinguish when philosophy and theology (and other literature dealing with religious thoughts) are separate or when one is of the other.

HSKL: Yes.

DTMR: Well, let me put forth that religion is of philosophy and that theology, and the expression of religious thought are a discipline of the philosophical realm. However, by no means is all philosophy of religion. The distinguishing factor is that religion deals with specific interior-originating experiences. These experiences pertain to faith. When experiences of faith (in God) are introduced to the work, it necessarily takes on the aspect of religion.

HSKL: The Bible deals with faith, yet it seems to me to be literature and does not seem to hold much of a philosophical air.

DTMR: That's correct. However, if we remember our analysis of philosophy, we will be able to understand that the Bible, being literature, takes on, as any other piece of literature, philosophical aspects the more interior-originating experiences are introduced into the work of art. Therefore, when the inner originating experience of faith is put forth, it not only takes on an aspect of philosophy, as it must necessarily do with the presence of an interior-originating experience, but also takes on the specific aspect of religion – or more accurately, religious philosophy, or in other terminology, theology.

HSKL: Well, if the Bible, because it deals with faith, should be considered to be philosophical, why do most people consider it to be a great work of literature?

DTMR: First, we must remember that all philosophy is of literary art and all literature has at least a smattering of the philosophical inherent within it, by virtue of the use of the interior-originating experience in literary art. The only distinction we can incorporate into the matter is that philosophy is a subdiscipline of literary art and, the means by which we may determine this sub-discipline is by the amount of interior-originating experiences that the work of art concerns itself with.

HSKL: I understand that.

DTMR: If this is understood, then we can quickly realize why most people see the Bible as a great work of literature.

HSKL: It is because the extent to which it deals with interior-originating experiences is the same general extent to which most other great works of literature deal with interior-originating experiences and does not deal with them to the degree in general that many of the great works of philosophy do. But, of course, it does make use, to a significant extent, of these interior-originating experiences (especially faith) and hence does take on philosophical aspects (specifically, religious philosophical aspects).

DTMR: I see you understand this matter perfectly.

HSKL: Thank you. But I think not entirely. A little bit ago, you said something curious. You mentioned that philosophy is a sub-discipline of literary art. Then, you said that the means by which we may determine the sub-discipline is by the amount of interior-originating experiences that are employed in the work of art.

DTMR: Yes, I recall that.

HSKL: You did not use the words "literary art" the second time. Are other forms of art considered to be works of philosophy? Can philosophy be expressed in other modes of communication besides the literary one?

DTMR: I don't see why not. As we determined before, a work of philosophy is only determined to be philosophical by the degree to which the work concerns itself with interior-originating experiences. Also, previously we have determined the expression of these experiences can take the form of different modes of communication – e.g., written, visual, structural. On the different modes of artistic expression, there is no limit as to the extent to which they may or may not concentrate or concern themselves with interior-originating experiences. Thus, it may be found that to the same degree that a work of written, philosophically oriented literary art is concerned, there may be an equivalent philosophically concerned work of art of the visual or structural kind; that is, there may be paintings or works of sculpture that are equally and to the same degree philosophical as a famous philosophical literary work of art. Thus, we may say that a certain painting or sculpture is of the philosophical just as we would say that Descartes' *Meditations* are of the philosophical.

HSKL: Yes, perfectly so.

DTMR: There is no difference except the means or mode of expression between the various arts.

HSKL: I see. You may not believe this, but at least for now, I have exhausted my reservoir of questions and will let you be at peace. Thank you for helping me. I appreciate the time you spent with me.

DTMR: Not at all. I enjoy these conversations immensely and look forward to any opportunity I might have to analyze topics such as we have discussed these past few days.

HSKL: Thank you very much. I'm glad to hear you say that because in my classes, various interesting problems come up and sometimes, they are not easily examined and solved.

DTMR: By all means, drop by again and we will take up whatever you have on your mind.

HSKL: Thank you. You can be sure I will take you up on that offer.

DTMR: Fine, Haskell. Study hard and good day!